Advance Praise for *Coping with Fears and Phobias*

'An excellent book, which should be interesting and beneficial to readers of a wide range of backgrounds.'

Anxious Times

'Impr... for those who w...

London

'A very valuable addition to the self-help literature. It is clear and concise, and gives plentiful, useful advice on how to use strategies derived from a cognitive behavioural framework to overcome anxiety.'

—*Ann Hackmann, Consultant Clinical Psychologist,*
Oxford University Department of Psychiatry

'Warren Mansell draws on a wealth of clinical experience to present an admirable combination of well-validated scientific strategies and a common-sense approach in his 10-step plan to coping with fears and phobias. Highly recommended.'

—*James Bennett-Levy,*
Oxford Cognitive Therapy Centre, University of Oxford

'Dr Mansell, who is internationally recognized for his research on fear and anxiety, provides a lucid, practical and realistic guide for those wishing to better understand and cope with their fears. It is the most helpful book on this topic I have read.'

—*Allison G. Harvey, Director, Sleep and Psychological*
Disorders Laboratory, University of California at Berkeley

'I highly recommend this valuable, thoughtful and exceptionally helpful book.'

—*Robert L. Leahy,*
Director, American Institute for Cognitive Therapy

'An excellent book which is easy to read and describes clearly the latest approaches in cognitive behaviour therapy.'

—*David Veale,*
Senior Lecturer at the Institute of Psychiatry, King's College London

Coping with
Fears and Phobias

A step-by-step guide to understanding and facing your anxieties

Warren Mansell

ONEWORLD

OXFORD

COPING WITH FEARS AND PHOBIAS

Published by Oneworld Publications 2007

Copyright © Warren Mansell 2007

ISBN-13: 978–1–85168–514–1

Typeset by Jayvee, Trivandrum, India
Cover design by Mungo Designs
Printed and bound by TJ International Ltd, Padstow, Cornwall

Oneworld Publications
185 Banbury Road
Oxford OX2 7AR
England
www.oneworld-publications.com

To download the worksheets, tables and diagrams
used in this book, and to access further information
on coping with your fears and phobias,
visit the *Coping with Fears and Phobias* mini-site:

www.oneworld-publications.com/fears

This book is dedicated to my mum and my dad, who have helped me to question and not to judge; my late grandma and my grandad (heading for his tenth decade!); and to Louise, who I love dearly.

Contents

Acknowledgements

This book would not be the same without the help, contributions and feedback from the following people: Stacey Lavda, Lorna Mansell, Angus MacDougall, Louise Dawson, Lorraine Morris, Annette Dawson, Tim Carey, Margaret Carey and Sam Cartwright Hatton. Thank you to 'No Panic' and their members who reviewed other self-help books for me in the early stages of developing this book. Thank you to Liz Hay for evaluating the book in a research study and thank you to the 'Reader' of an earlier manuscript of this book for all the helpful suggestions. Many people have influenced the ideas in this book, and I am indebted to their work. They are David M. Clark, Paul Salkovskis, Adrian Wells, Anke Ehlers, Tim Carey, Bill Powers, Tony Morrison, Allison Harvey, Ed Watkins, Roz Shafran, Emily Holmes, Dan Freeman, Craig Steel, Sara Tai, Ian Lowens, Paul Gilbert, Ann Hackmann, Gillian Butler, Steve Hayes, John Kabat-Zinn, Mark Williams, John Teasdale, Richard Bentall, Tim Beck and David Burns. The British Association of Behavioural and Cognitive Psychotherapies and its annual conference organised by Philip Tata, Rod Holland and their team have provided the opportunity for many of these great thinkers and therapists to share their most recent and innovative ideas with the rest of us. Thank you to Steve Jones, Juliet Mabey and Kate Kirkpatrick for developing this great series of books and so giving me the opportunity to write a self-help book of this kind.

Series Foreword

This series is intended to provide clear, accessible, and practical information to individuals with a wide range of psychological disorders, as well as to their friends, relatives and interested professionals. As the causes of emotional distress can be complex, books in this series are not designed purely to detail self-treatment information. Instead, each volume sets out to offer guidance on the relevant, evidence-based psychological approaches that are available for the particular condition under discussion. Where appropriate, suggestions are also given on how to apply particular aspects of those techniques that can be incorporated into self-help approaches. Equally important, readers are offered information on which forms of therapy are likely to be beneficial, enabling sufferers to make informed decisions about treatment options with their referring clinician.

Each book also considers aspects of the disorder that are likely to be relevant to each individual's experience of receiving treatment, including the therapeutic approaches of medical professionals, the nature of diagnosis, and the myths that might surround a particular disorder. General issues that can also affect a sufferer's quality of life, such as stigma, isolation, self-care and relationships are also covered in many of the volumes.

The books in this series are not intended to replace therapists, since many individuals will need a personal treatment programme from a qualified clinician. However, each title offers individually tailored strategies, devised by highly experienced practicing clinicians, predominantly based on the latest techniques of cognitive behavioural therapy, which have been shown to be extremely effective in changing the way sufferers think about themselves and their problems. In addition, titles also include a variety of practical features such as rating scales and diary sheets, helpful case studies drawn from real life, and a wide range of up-to-date resources including self-help groups, recommended reading, and useful websites. Consequently, each book provides the necessary materials for sufferers to become active participants in their own care, enabling constructive engagement with clinical professionals when needed and, when appropriate, to take independent action.

Dr Steven Jones
Series Editor

1

Is this book for you?

Courage is not the lack of fear. It is acting in spite of it.

Mark Twain

Fear is a normal emotion. We all experience fear when we are in danger, but it usually subsides when we have reached safety. However, fear can also be so extreme and persistent that it disrupts people's lives and prevents them from doing what they want to do. In this book, I will try to provide you with enough information about fear itself, and how to cope with it that you can begin to reclaim your life. I am going to approach this topic both in my role as a health professional with experience in treating anxiety disorders, and just as importantly, as a fellow human being. Fear can blight our lives and often returns when you least expect it. Yet, I have seen that it is possible for people to learn to cope better with it each time.

Many people learn to cope better with their phobias and some will even fully recover from them. However, the path can be slow and include setbacks. This book will not rush you into doing things quickly. It will not force you to confront all of your worst fears. It is important for people to change at a pace they are happy with, and the process of learning to cope with fear is no different. You are in control.

What are fears and phobias?

I will say it again: fear is a normal emotion. It is a vital way for us to protect ourselves. We all experience fear from time to time. Some people experience fear much more than others, often for very understandable reasons. It is normal to try to escape from danger and seek safety, and people often do it for very good reasons. Looking both ways before you cross the road is a good example. I will explain in more detail later exactly what fear involves, including the way it affects your thinking, behaviour and physiology. The more that you know about fear, the better equipped you will be to deal with it.

People have attempted to define phobias in many different ways. In essence, a phobia is a fear that disrupts a person's life. For example, nearly everyone fears being physically injured, but only some people alter their lives because of this fear, for example by not going out of the house or avoiding crowded places. The amount of disruption is what distinguishes a phobia from a fear, but what causes this fear is complicated and varies between different people. I will try to explain this later.

Some people have proposed that phobias are 'irrational fears'. However, this way of defining a phobia has proved to be unreliable and not particularly helpful. Who is to say what is rational or irrational? I wouldn't like to make that kind of judgement about somebody else. I'm fully aware that I'm not rational all the time, and I'm happy not to be. So, this book will focus on the most important target – reclaiming your life from the phobia, regardless of whether people believe that the phobia is irrational or not.

Experiences you may have had

People who suffer from problems with their anxiety have often had some unusual or frightening experiences that they cannot explain, such as trembling or heart palpitations. Other examples include distressing thoughts about future dangers, memories that come back to you over and over again, and physical sensations such as aches, pains, light headedness and exhaustion. Many more of these experiences are listed in appendix 1 of the book. They are placed there so that you can refer to them when you need them, and when you feel comfortable with reading about them. Alongside each experience is an explanation of what it is, and an everyday explanation for why it might occur. If you have had any of these experiences then you are likely to find this book helpful.

Who could benefit from this book?

Fear works in the same way for everybody because we all have the same basic biology. So there is good reason to expect that this book can help anyone who wants to cope better with their fears. I would expect that people with a very specific phobia, or people with many different phobias and anxieties, will pick up useful information and techniques from this guide. People with anxiety conditions that are caused by trauma, such as post-traumatic stress disorder (PTSD) may also find it helpful, in addition to people whose anxieties come out as obsessive thoughts or rituals. Also, it provides help in coping with anxiety regardless of whether a phobia is your main difficulty or not. In particular, I would expect people with a diagnosis of a serious psychological disorder reading this book to learn as much about how to cope with their anxiety as a person with no diagnosis at all. Appendix 2 lists the kinds of problems that may be helped by the approach of this book.

There are, however, some essentials needed to benefit from this book. First, appropriate reading skills are necessary. People with difficulties with reading, for any reason, may find it helpful for a friend, family member or health professional to work through the book with them. Second, you need to identify a fear, phobia or anxiety as a cause of problems in your life. Although this book would be helpful to anyone with other more serious difficulties, it does mainly tackle fear, phobias and anxiety, and so effects would be expected mainly in this area. Third, learning to cope with a fear needs to be one of your current priorities. For example, it would not be helpful for a person to start reading this book when having to deal with an immediate emergency. However, as soon as there is some space in your day to focus on and read a short section, even if it is for just ten minutes, it may begin to provide some help.

Finally, it is worth saying that nearly everyone who experiences a phobia or distressing anxiety seems to have had the thought at times: 'I am different – what works for other people will not work for me!' It is very likely that you will have this thought when you read this book. Now, I certainly cannot guarantee that everything in this book will be directly relevant to you. In fact, this would be very unlikely – the book is written with all kinds of fears and phobias in mind. One person with a phobia rarely understands another person who has a different phobia; to each of them the other person's fears seem illogical or unbelievable. Yet, this book will try to point out the similarities between different people who are anxious, rather than the differences. In my experience, many people who have managed to cope with their fears have at one time had the thought that they are somehow the exception. If you were to believe this it would certainly be an easy way to justify not reading any further and putting off trying to face your fears for another day. But how helpful would this be in the long run? Is it worth thinking that you cannot be helped, if you don't know whether or not it is true and this thought makes you feel worse about yourself? What have you got to lose by reading on and seeing if some of the ideas in the book might apply to you? My suggestion is to try them out, and then you can make your own mind up.

This book is just one of many sources of support. It is not a substitute for other support in any way. I encourage you to look into different ways of getting support, information and treatment. Chapter 12 provides advice about accessing local sources of support and treatment, and the appendices provide lists of self-help groups, websites, and other useful contacts. It is up to you to draw on what you think might be helpful for you. No treatment is going to be perfect, but if you have more information about what is available, you can make better decisions about what might be helpful for you.

This book provides information to take in, and techniques to try out. In this way, it tries to balance changes in thinking with changes in behaviour. The two are intertwined. First there is some background information on phobias and how to deal with them. Then, in chapter 3, I provide some practical techniques to get started. The following chapters provide more information on the nature of fear, the way that 'vicious cycles' develop, and how to prepare for change. Then, subsequent chapters describe how to go about putting self-help into practice and encourage you to begin to try out some techniques. I also focus on dealing with the consequences of phobias, what to do when you feel that the techniques are not working, and some more general advice on how to move your life forward in the way you want. The book has several appendices that you can refer to when necessary, including record sheets, exercises, a list of diagnoses, and a list of fears with non-threatening explanations. Many of the chapters include personal accounts to illustrate the main points, and there is a summary of key points at the end of each chapter to consolidate what has been covered.

Finally, there is a companion website to this guide that you can access at any time:

www.oneworld-publications.com/fears

There is no need to rush in reading this book. It is more important to check that you have fully digested what you have read and decided whether you agree with it. At first, just read through and think about whether you agree with what is being said. See if some of what you read prompts you to think about your fears in a different way. Then, when you are ready, you might choose to try out some of the recommendations in the book and see if they work for you. It is not a problem if they don't work the first time round. You may have to try them out a few times before they work for you. You are likely to find that new ways of thinking or behaving take time to 'click'.

It is probably better to try to work through the book from start to finish, but there may be certain sections you want to focus on, because they are more relevant at the time. It may be worth preparing yourself for the fact that not all of the elements of the book will apply to you, and to all of your experiences. Everyone is unique. But hopefully a large part of it will. Please try to carry on when you feel a section does not apply to you until you get to a section that does. You can always come back to that section later if you want. I would hope that you could maximise the usefulness of the book by focusing first on the things that definitely ring true for you, and then maybe revisit the other sections later.

When you do read the book, try to focus all your attention on it, but don't get too immersed in it either. Probably half an hour a day is the most you would want to read it, but ten minutes is enough. It is probably better to read it for a short while at a time over many days or weeks than to read it for several hours all at once and then not return to it. At the end of the day, it is only a book, and you need to get on with your everyday life without a book interfering too much.

Clearly it is not possible for you to have a very real relationship with the author of a self-help book. I can't respond in writing to what you are thinking right now. However, the style of this book is designed to be collaborative. I am aiming to introduce you to certain ideas and techniques, but leaving it up to you to decide whether they apply to you or are helpful. I am trying to share my own experiences and those of some of my clients, to make the point that many of us have similar experiences and we can learn from each other. I have put the work into writing this book (but not lost sleep over it!), but you need to put the work in to read what it says, evaluate it, and try the suggestions (again in a reasonable way – you have plenty of other things to read and think about!). The idea is that the work is roughly equal and the balance of power is roughly equal – don't believe anything written here until you have considered it and tried it out.

'Coping with anxiety' versus 'overcoming anxiety' – are they the same or different?

This book is part of the *Coping with ...* series by Oneworld Publications, and so its emphasis is on 'coping'. Other books emphasise 'overcoming' or even 'triumphing' over anxiety. What is the difference? I prefer 'coping with anxiety' as a goal for this book, because it reminds us that some anxiety can be normal. Eliminating anxiety completely is certainly not a goal of this book. So, getting better is about coping with anxiety better. Nevertheless, it would be possible for some people reading this book, or through other means, to 'overcome' their anxiety problems eventually – meaning that their anxiety no longer plagues and preoccupies them, nor has a significant impact on the way they want to live their lives. My hunch is that some readers of the book will want to take a 'coping' approach and some will want to take an 'overcoming' approach. It is up to you. However, whichever approach you wish to take, the general message is the same: people can learn to cope with anxiety over time and, despite setbacks along the way, many of them will overcome the negative effects of anxiety on their lives.

A note on Cognitive Behavioural Therapy (CBT)

You have probably heard about CBT. Like any new treatment, it can generate a lot of opinions, both good and bad. CBT has been shown to be effective in a number of trials, but it is not perfect, and it is not always the same when it is carried out by different people. You may have had CBT and already benefited from it. You may have been trying to get CBT and be frustrated that it is not available locally. Or you may have had CBT and not feel that you have benefited. All of these experiences are common. This book takes a CBT approach because studies show it is more effective than other treatments available for anxiety and phobias. CBT informs how I practice therapy, along with influences from other psychological approaches, and it appears to work well with my clients. So, I encourage you to have an open mind and see what there is in this book that you can use to your advantage, and don't feel that you have to agree with everything. Again, you are in control and only you can decide what is going to be helpful for you.

Key points

A summary appears at the end of each chapter, this is designed to highlight the key points and help consolidate what has been covered. If you find that you don't agree with some of the statements, or they are unclear, then it may help to go back through the chapter. Other points may become clearer as you read further.

- Fear is a normal emotion.
- Many people learn to cope better with their phobias.
- It is important for people to change at a pace they are happy with.
- The more that you know about fear, the better equipped you will be to deal with it.
- Fear works in the same way for everyone because we have the same fundamental biology.
- Ultimately, only you can decide what is going to be helpful for you.

2

Who gets phobias and how do they learn to cope?

Although the world is full of suffering, it is also full of the overcoming of it.

Helen Keller

Fears and phobias are very common. There are seven major categories of anxiety disorders, they are: specific phobia, panic disorder, agoraphobia, social phobia, obsessive-compulsive disorder (OCD), post-traumatic stress disorder (PTSD) and generalised anxiety disorder (GAD) (definitions are provided in appendix 2). Estimating exactly how many people experience anxiety disorders is difficult because it depends how it is measured. Anxiety conditions vary on a sliding scale like height or weight, from relatively mild to moderate to severe. For example, one large study of over 8000 people in the general population found that nearly half of all the people interviewed reported having at least one unreasonably strong fear. For around one in every five people, these fears reflect a condition that creates significant disruption at some point in their lives.

An example in this category would be a fear of closed spaces (claustrophobia) that leads a person to avoid a range of situations (for example, lifts, traffic jams, buses and trains), that limits their life and leads to frustration from friends and family. Some of the more severe anxiety conditions are less common, at around one person in twenty. An example in this category would be a person who could only make infrequent trips from the house for fear of collapse. Your own fears may lie in any one of these categories. Whether your condition is mild, moderate or severe, you are certainly not alone in being affected by fear.

The very fact that phobias are so common should make it easy to appreciate that phobias can affect anyone. They affect people from both sexes, from all races and cultures. It is not possible to identify one particular kind of person as being more vulnerable to phobias. The vignettes on these pages provide an idea of the wide range of people who experience phobias. As you can see, they are often people who show great strength and intellect in other areas of their lives. Even the most rational and capable people can experience phobias.

Personal example of a phobia – Rasheeda

> I am a research assistant at a university. I have been terrified of spiders since I was a child. I always asked for somebody's help if I saw a spider. I never really thought I could cope on my own. This resulted in me becoming very anxious over what I would do if I saw a big spider when alone, how would I get rid of it? Who could I ask for help? The anxiety that I would find a spider when no one was around to help me meant that I thought about and checked around me for spiders a good portion of the day and I had sleepless nights. It was really affecting my life and that's why this fear was a problem.

Personal example of a phobia – Alice

I have a form of agoraphobia which limits the distance I can travel from my home. This means that I am okay shopping and working in my immediate area but I cannot travel further than about eight miles without feeling extremely anxious. This is itself an achievement because once I could not travel more than a mile. My phobia limits my ability to see family and friends, and going away on holiday is impossible. It is as if there is a wall around the perimeter of the area I can travel. My work as a teacher and private tutor has been limited by my fears, but I manage to work locally.

Personal example of generalised anxiety and post-traumatic stress disorder – Paul

I have always been an anxious person and a worrier. I think it goes back to how I was treated at home. My dad would use physical violence to discipline me, and I never knew when I was going to get hit next. I left home in my early twenties and I seemed to cope OK with my worries for a while. But a few years ago I was assaulted at work by one of the other postal workers – it was completely out of the blue – he was drunk and he thought that I had bad-mouthed him. This attack made me scared of getting attacked again, but not just at work – near where I lived too – I was on edge all the time. I got flashbacks of the attack, and I couldn't get it out of my mind – trying to tell myself it hadn't happened. I went to see my GP and she said I had post-traumatic stress disorder (PTSD). I got some medication for it, but it didn't help that much because I couldn't stop thinking about what had happened.

Personal example of a phobia – Janet

I believe that my anxiety problems started when my mother died. Before this time, I had always enjoyed my own company, and shopping trips had never been a problem. But around twenty years ago, my mother died suddenly, alone at home. At the time, I was a young mother of two children. It was a stressful period of my life, especially when later on my father reacted by neglecting himself and drinking heavily; I would find him at home in some awful states. After my mother died, I found that I kept cleaning and sorting out drawers and putting things in order, in case I died suddenly too. I was worrying a lot about dying round this time. One day, I was in a supermarket and all of a sudden I couldn't remember what to buy. This was odd, but I met up with a friend to have a coffee and cigarette, and I was actually laughing about it for a while, but then at the checkout I just couldn't count the money in my hand. It took three attempts to get it right! I got increasingly anxious, and so I had to leave. I can't even remember getting home; just the relief when I was home and the house door closed and I was safe. After that, I was focusing on whether it may happen again and I was just waiting for it, especially if I was on a shopping trip alone.

Personal example of experiencing anxiety, depression and physical problems – Laura

I have had anxiety, depression and many phobias. I have had claustrophobia, been afraid of dying, choking, going blind or deaf, and having a chronic illness such as Alzheimers or Motor Neurone Disease. I currently have diagnoses of ME and anaemia. My physical symptoms of pains, creepy numbness, tingling, swallowing difficulties and tiredness are with me for much of the time, and when they are at full force I feel called at their mercy. But they can be severe and chronic for several weeks and then some of them can suddenly disappear. It is a very perplexing and frightening state of mind to be in.

What does it mean to be diagnosed with an anxiety disorder?

It is very natural for people to want to work out what is wrong with them when they feel anxious and it has such a major impact on their lives. When we get physical symptoms of illness we want to know the cause so that we can receive the appropriate treatment. For the same reason, people get diagnosed with anxiety 'disorders'. A diagnosis of an anxiety 'disorder' works in a similar way. The patient lists their symptoms, for example, panic attacks coming out of the blue, worrying about panicking, and the doctor provides a label for it – 'panic disorder'. It seems that the label can have both a positive and negative impact.

On the positive side, it can help a person to realise their experiences are a normal reaction to an extreme life event, or series of life events. For example, we know that post-traumatic stress disorder (PTSD) is triggered by a trauma such as an assault or natural disaster. So, people with PTSD can often realise that their distressing experiences such as vivid memories and feeling 'on edge' all of the time are a normal reaction to an out-of-the-ordinary experience. There is good evidence that intense emotional experiences like traumas lead to strongly encoded memories. So, these experiences do not mean that the person is 'going mad'. Indeed, most people get these symptoms in the immediate aftermath of a trauma, but typically they seem to fade away within a few months.

Another positive effect of the 'disorder' label, is that it helps a person to explain some of their unusual behaviour to themselves and to people around them. So, rather than being deliberate or one's own fault, these reactions are seen as effects of the disorder that are very difficult for a person to control. It is very understandable for people to react in unusual ways at the peaks of intense anxiety when there do not seem any alternatives for them. Nevertheless, eventually people can learn to manage these moods and behaviours more successfully.

One of the negative effects of the label is that it sometimes provides a false sense that a person's problems are completely understood. Having the label 'anxiety disorder' can also make us believe that we know what is causing our problems and how they can be treated. 'Why are you anxious?' is answered, 'Because of my panic disorder' – but really the panic disorder is not the cause – it is a description of the symptoms. The causes are more complicated (and will be covered in chapter 4), but put simply, there is no single cause of an anxiety disorder. This leads to a further problem with diagnosis. Some health professionals and researchers are convinced that anxiety conditions, like obsessive-compulsive disorder (OCD), are similar to certain diagnosed physical diseases – that the conditions are caused by a person's genes and the problems are therefore out of the person's control and can only be treated with medication. While genes contribute to the chances of a person being anxious (genes also contribute to all kinds of other personal qualities like whether a person is religious or not!), it is misleading to think that they are the only cause. And many problems with an influence from genes are not treated with medication – short-sightedness is managed using spectacles, and proneness to heart disease is best managed by exercise and improved diet.

A final problem with diagnosing disorders is that people are not normally afraid of just one thing – they may have many fears. For example, a person who has 'dental phobia' may actually be afraid of several different things – being in an enclosed space, injections and not being in control of the situation. This makes it seem as though they have lots of different 'disorders'. However, it is much simpler to think that certain ways that people think and behave can make them afraid of lots of things. If you are someone who always thinks the worst of any difficult situation, then you might become afraid of many different bad things happening. So it is simpler to think of these styles of thinking and behaving rather than adding up all of the different things a person is afraid of. The good news is that the same ways of coping with one fear can be applied, with a little tweaking, to another fear. So, recovery can progress and spread to different areas over time.

If you have one or more diagnoses of anxiety disorders, then what you can be sure of is that your fears, whatever they are, are very distressing to you and are getting in the way of how you want to live your life. This book will try to introduce you to the ways of treating yourself, thinking and behaving that can reduce the impact of your anxiety. For the sake of reference and interest the different phobias and anxiety disorders are listed in appendix 2, alongside their key characteristics. It is up to you whether you adopt a disorder label for your anxiety problems, considering both the good and bad points that were covered above. Whatever the case, it is most likely that you will be helped by developing a more personal understanding of what keeps your own anxiety problems going, and using this to learn to cope better over time.

Fears and phobias associated with other mental health problems

Anxiety is not restricted to people who have traditional 'anxiety disorders'. For example, people with 'eating disorders' such as anorexia nervosa or bulimia nervosa are often afraid of becoming overweight and unsightly and restrict their eating to try to prevent this from happening. People with concerns that they have a serious illness, like cancer, that their doctor has not identified may seek lots of reassurance from their friends, family and GP, and even get several specialist tests that prove negative, yet remain unconvinced that they do not have an illness. Many people who have experienced a serious 'breakdown' (such as mania, depression or psychosis) are afraid that it will happen again and do many things to try hard to prevent another breakdown.

There is now evidence that people with each of the concerns above have very similar styles of thinking and behaving as people with 'anxiety disorders'. So, this book takes the approach that people with any concern which frightens and preoccupies them can learn to cope in a similar way. These 'disorders' clearly seem different and affect different kinds of people, but the things that keep them going are very similar. Please see appendix 2 for some other examples.

Recovery from phobias

The length of time that a person can suffer from a phobia varies widely. The average is around ten years, but this figure hides the fact that some people can experience a phobia for their whole lives whereas other people may have an acute phobia lasting one or two years. However, whatever the duration of a phobia, it is never too late to change. People who have been anxious all their lives can learn to cope with their fears. Rasheeda's recovery provides one example.

Rasheeda's recovery

I think it is hard to believe before starting therapy that there is any chance of success. Being afraid of spiders had become part of who I was. I was arachnophobic. I thought it was out of my control. One important thing I learnt in therapy is that recovery is a process and it doesn't happen overnight. At the very start sometimes I felt disheartened but it definitely paid off to persist. Once I started to feel there was progress being made, it was like a small breakthrough and the recovery process sped up considerably. I managed to slowly do

Continued

> things that I never dreamt I could do before, like put a cup over a spider. The biggest relief I have experienced since I have had therapy is the fact that I am no longer worried all the time about the possibility that I may encounter a spider, and I no longer spend most of my day thinking about and checking for them. This is because I now know I can cope on my own.

What does learning to cope involve?

In the next chapter I will describe some simple coping strategies. Before turning to them, it may be helpful to consider the main features of coping.

1. *Coping does not involve having to face extreme anxiety.* Much of learning to cope involves understanding more and therefore not facing feelings of anxiety at all. Another part of learning to cope does involve facing these feelings, but you will be partly prepared for this even before you start. When you do come to face the physical feelings of anxiety, you can do it a little at a time. In fact, facing fears a little at a time is proven to be effective. Only when you feel comfortable with each step do you move on. And when you do, it is your choice. At no time during reading this book will you be made to experience extreme anxiety.

2. *Coping does involve facing and understanding the source of your fears, and tolerating some unpleasant feelings.* In order to cope with something that makes you feel distressed, it is helpful to know what it is that you are trying to cope with. To take a colourful example, a knight whose challenge is to slay a fierce dragon would want to find out about the beast, where it lived, what its strengths and vulnerabilities were, before setting out on his quest. So, learning to deal with a phobia is about learning about the object of your fears. While it may not be necessary to go through extreme

anxiety to learn to cope better, it will be necessary to experience some bodily feelings that may seem unpleasant at first. However, the more you learn about anxiety, the more you will realise that these feelings are not dangerous in themselves, and are actually a sign that your body is working as it should do. With this information, you can begin to tolerate these feelings as you make forward steps. If you cannot face the idea of ever facing unpleasant bodily feelings, then that is OK for now. You can read about them first, and take your own time to decide whether you want to face them. The choice of path to recovery is your own.

3. *Coping does not involve making an enormous effort.* Coping does involve commitment to opening your mind to new ideas, and to coming to a decision about whether you are ready to change. It does involve starting to think about things differently from how you have done in the past. But it does not involve pushing yourself really hard. This is not a contest or a race. You don't have to struggle to cope with fear. You might have tried struggling really hard already, and that is not surprising. If you've had your fears for a long time and they have led to all kinds of troubles, it is very understandable that you can get frustrated and worked up. We are often brought up being told to make an enormous effort to solve our problems. We can all do it. Yet, has it worked up until now? Maybe on occasion but not in the long run? Later I will explain more about why struggling with our fears seems not to work. This book will not advocate a Herculean struggle with your fears, but it will encourage you to be open-minded and committed to reading and trying out what is suggested in your own time.

4. *Coping is about being kind to yourself.* You have already read up to this point in the book. That is good. You are well beyond the start of the book, and showing a commitment to

read further. To some people it may seem unnecessary to provide praise for reading a few pages of a book. It is not like you have run a marathon. Yet, this is still a good step. If you can continue to praise yourself in this way, you should find the whole experience of working through this book more pleasant. You don't need to go over the top and tell yourself you are fantastic, but simply acknowledging each step is good in itself. When things don't go as planned, it is often tempting for people to criticise themselves, telling themselves they are stupid for doing the wrong thing. They almost think that they can punish themselves into doing better next time. Again, does this work? You might have tried it, and I would bet that it doesn't work in the long run. More to the point, would you want to behave in this way to someone else who you care for, like a friend or a child? If not, then what makes you so different? In this book, I will advocate being kind to yourself, praising yourself for a job well done, and giving yourself the benefit of the doubt when things don't work out quite as planned. There will probably be a good reason for this, and you may well be able to work out the reason by using this book. Telling yourself you are no good would simply get in the way of that process. It is not helpful. Some examples of alternative ways to treat yourself are provided in chapter 3.

5. *Coping is about understanding what goes on in your own mind and then making your own choices.* When a person is very distressed and panicky, people who care for them will often want to help that person immediately. When other people understand the cause of the distress, this can be helpful – when children fall over and hurt themselves, their parents might help by washing the wound and putting on a plaster. However, it seems that the distress of fears and phobias is very often caused by experiences that only the sufferer can detect because they are inside the body or the mind. Some

examples are upsetting thoughts and unusual bodily sensations. The first step to coping with anxieties about experiences inside us is to understand what is going on in our own minds. You are in the best position to know this. No expert on this planet knows exactly what is going on in your mind as well as you do. This book will give you some clues and provide you with some of the questions to ask yourself. However, you are the person who is in the privileged position to understand yourself better and then eventually to take steps to help yourself recover.

6. *Coping is about drawing on your strengths and qualities.* To learn to cope with a fear, it is necessary to admit the fear exists, to begin to face it and try to understand it. Sometimes people do not realise that they already have some solid foundations to begin to cope already. For example, your ability to sit down and concentrate long enough to read some of this book is a strength in itself. So is the decision to face up to your fear, even for a short time. In my experience, people typically underestimate, or play down, the strengths that they can draw upon to cope with their fears. So, one of my suggestions is to notice these qualities. Once you can notice your personal qualities, you can begin to develop them. It is rather like exercising a muscle. There are many strengths that you may be asked to notice, draw upon, or develop in the course of this book. Some examples of strengths, qualities and resources are provided in the table at the end of chapter 11.

How Janet tried to cope with her phobia

> On journeys, I would take my own tapes of music I liked, which reminded me of people I knew and places I loved. Because of my dry mouth I took a bottle of water with me. I

Continued

also decided that if I felt uncomfortable on my way, it was OK for me to turn around and go home. I had so many conversations with myself in my head, that this wasn't always possible. But when it was, I could go home. I had a choice. I longed to visit a friend in Ireland. But because public transport had become a problem as well, I thought I would never do it. So I started to make shorter visits on the coach and train to see my Aunt in Blackpool. I felt a wreck – loaded with tapes, CDs and books and my water – but it gradually got easier. On my first journey to Blackpool I arrived safe. I had not fainted or died on the bus. I was determined I wanted to go to Ireland eventually.

Seven helpful beliefs

It can be helpful to plot how you are doing over the course of this programme. There are many scales that measure anxiety and people's ability to cope with it. The one below is adapted from a colleague and friend of mine, Sam Cartwright-Hatton. I will introduce it here so that you can see where you are starting from – your 'baseline'. The idea is that as you begin to cope better, you will gradually increase your belief in these statements. You could start by rating how much you believe each of these statements today, by heading a column with the date, and putting in a rating from 0 to 100 for each belief. So you may not believe these statements at all, in which case put 0, or you might believe it a little (say 10 or 20), right up to 100 if you are 100 per cent sure. Then, at regular intervals, over weeks or months, you can complete the following columns. How regularly you complete them will depend on the timescale that seems right for your programme, and your opportunities to put it into practice.

Table 2.1 Seven Helpful Beliefs

	Date	Date	Date
The world is quite a safe place for me			
I can cope with most things that happen			
I am kind to myself when I make a mistake			
I can accept the feelings that I have			
I can deal with being unsure about things			
I tend not to worry that much			
I know other people who like and respect me			

A blank copy of this table is available online.

Key points

- People with phobias often show great strength and intellect in other areas of their lives.
- Whatever the duration of a phobia, it is never too late to change.
- Facing fears a little at a time is proven to be effective.
- Learning to cope does not involve pushing yourself really hard.
- Coping is about being kind to yourself.
- Coping is about drawing on your strengths and qualities.
- Just a few ways of thinking and behaving can explain why some people have lots of different fears.
- It can be helpful to apply the same ways of coping with one fear to another fear.

3

Some key coping strategies to begin with

Let us not look back in anger or forward in fear, but around in awareness.

James Thurber

This book is designed to gear you up gradually into coping with your anxiety. However, you may want to know what you can do right now. In this section, I describe some strategies that you can start to use immediately, and will return to later in the book. They are quite easy to try out, but more difficult to put into practice regularly. In fact, you may find that it takes a while to get into a pattern of doing them regularly, and many people without any problems with anxiety would find them difficult to do consistently. Don't let this put you off – just a little practise of these techniques can be helpful.

Slow, shallow breathing

The idea of using this technique may sound like a cliché – just breathing slowly and with shallow breaths. However, there is an important scientific reason why it works. When we feel anxious, our body responds in a variety of ways to help us escape a danger. To understand this, it is helpful to go back a long way, before our present day society.

During our evolutionary past, escape might have involved running away from a predator at great speed. So our body has evolved to prepare for this type of escape. One way it does this is to increase our rate and depth of breathing – *hyperventilation*. This provides air to provide fuel for our muscles, so that we can run faster. However, in modern times, when people become anxious they often have no reason to expend a lot of energy. For example, if you were to feel very anxious about a meeting with your boss, it would not be helpful to sprint away from the office as fast as possible. So, when we get anxious we breathe faster and deeper, but we don't actually use up the oxygen. This is not dangerous in any way. Yet we can feel its effects. Hyperventilation leads to odd feelings that vary between different people. Some people report that it makes them feel more anxious. Many people describe it as feeling 'unreal', 'floaty' or 'spacey'. You may have experienced this feeling. Sometimes people think that this feeling means something more dangerous, like they are about to faint, or have a heart attack. However, it is not that complicated. It is simply the result of breathing too fast and too deeply. After breathing normally for a while, the body uses up the extra oxygen and the feeling passes (strictly speaking, this effect is the decrease of carbon dioxide in the bloodstream rather than an increase in the amount of oxygen – it is called 'alkalosis'; when muscles are active, the oxygen is converted to carbon dioxide, but with increased hyperventilation, this oxygen converts to carbon dioxide at a much slower rate). Many people seem to think that 'taking a deep breath' is a way of calming themselves before an anxiety-provoking situation. But this is another example of taking in more oxygen than you need. Doing slow, shallow breathing is an alternative that doesn't lead to hyperventilation. So how do you do it?

Janet's experience of hyperventilation

> Traffic lights were a problem for me if they went red before I got to them. A particular set of lights became the worst for me, because on one occasion I had stopped and the traffic was very bad. I suddenly felt that I couldn't breathe, and so I was gasping for breath. I then became light-headed and I wanted to get out of the car and leave it there. Afterwards, I stopped going that way for many years, unless someone was with me. I would worry and lose sleep for days, often cancelling or making up an excuse not to go. When my son started college I felt that I had to go through those lights, but my heart would race, my mouth would go dry, and my breathing was laboured just at the thought of going. So I would take a two mile detour to avoid them. Now, I realise that when I had thought about driving through these lights I must have been breathing differently, leading me to feel light-headed and then fear that I would faint in public. I didn't know then about the unusual but harmless effects of hyperventilating.

There is no special secret to slow, shallow breathing itself, and any attempt to breathe more slowly and lightly is likely to help. However, it can be split into stages to make it easier to practice.

1. *Notice that you are hyperventilating.* This is probably the most important stage, and not easy for anyone. To start slow, shallow breathing you have to first notice that you are not doing it. As a rule, when you notice that you are feeling more anxious than usual, try to focus on your breathing. Take your attention from whatever it is you were focusing on (such as your worries) and focus it onto your breathing. You can notice this in your chest movements or in the air moving through your nose. Feel the air going in and out.

2. *Slow down.* Once you have noticed your breathing, begin to take control. Slow it down, while still focusing on your body.

Are you still breathing deeply? Reduce the amount of air that you breathe in, so you are taking small, shallow breaths. To get the pace right, it may help to do the following: breathe in, hold it and count 'one thousand, two thousand' slowly in your head, breathe out and count 'one thousand, two thousand' slowly in your head, and repeat again. Once you have got this pace, then stop the counting but continue breathing at this rate. It is about two seconds between each breath in and out. Keep it shallow – this is not about taking deep breaths.

3. *Return to what you are doing.* Once you have slowed your breathing down to this pace, you can now return your attention to what you were doing. Try to focus on your surroundings, rather than on the thoughts in your head.

Some people seem to breathe faster and hyperventilate because they are convinced that they are suffocating. So, one concern that people have when they are breathing more slowly and lightly, is that they might suffocate. Fortunately this is not possible, as the body automatically forces us to take enough breaths – no one has ever killed themselves from just holding their breath! So, if you have this concern, then this is actually a good reason to try slow breathing. It provides you with a way to test out this belief. If you can manage it, and the slower and lighter the better, it shows that you will not suffocate.

The slow breathing technique is also used as part of 'brief mindfulness relaxation'(detailed next). In both, the key is to notice that you are breathing too fast at that moment and catch it, and take a brief moment (as little as a minute) to focus on your breathing and slow it down. It also provides a brief release from worrying chains of thoughts, and gives you a chance to step outside them. Try it out next time you have a big increase in your anxiety. If it doesn't work for you, then that's OK, there are other ways to help – but if it does help, it will come in handy in the future. Don't try to slow breathe all the time though, as this would be to suggest that it is more important than it really is. Just use it when and if you think it might help.

Brief mindfulness relaxation

Brief mindfulness relaxation, while not a treatment in itself, can be used as a coping strategy. I will call it BMR from now on. It is related to approaches that have been introduced from meditation into therapy recently by people such as John Kabat-Zinn, John Teasdale and Mark Williams, and from a different line of thought, Adrian Wells. There are two points to make about BMR before describing how to do it.

First, unlike slow breathing, BMR is something you do whether or not you are feeling anxious at the time. People who do BMR typically find a certain time in the day to do it regularly, for example after lunch or dinner each day.

Second, unlike slow breathing, there is no agreement as to why BMR helps people, or even what its purpose is. People do not do it to feel better. So it is tempting to ask, what is the point? Well, people who do it regularly do seem to cope better with their anxiety. The leading theory for why it works is that it changes people's relationship with their thoughts. They learn to notice their thoughts, feelings and memories as they go through their mind, and accept them as part of their mind. Nothing more and nothing less. Most of us do exactly the opposite. We struggle with our thoughts, feelings and memories, trying to block them out or change them. BMR provides a brief moment in the day when you don't do that – a break from the continual struggle with your own mind.

To try BMR, follow the instructions below:

1. *Timing and location.* BMR can be carried out anywhere. However, certain things make it easier. It is best to start doing it at a time when you can guarantee that you have

some space in your day, and that you are unlikely to be interrupted. To begin with, it is best to start in a location that is
reasonably quiet, and in a place that you feel relatively comfortable. When you first begin, just set a brief amount of
time to try it, as little as five minutes. It is better to do BMR
well for a brief amount of time than to struggle to do it for a
long period. It is up to you whether you do BMR with your
eyes open or closed. Some people prefer to begin by closing
their eyes, but it can also be done with the eyes open.

2. *Focus on one thing at a time.* BMR involves focusing on one
experience at a time. Traditionally, people focus on their
breathing mainly because our breathing is something that
we have with us all the time. However, you can choose to
focus on something else, such as a sound outside. For
example if you were in a field you might focus on the bird-
song, or if you were sitting at home you might choose to
focus on the sound of your central heating. The key is to
choose one thing to focus on, try to keep your attention on
it, and, when you get distracted from it by a thought or
another feeling or sound, return your focus to that object
again. It is probably better for the object of attention to be
quite simple so that you can practise focusing for long
periods – loud music or a television programme don't quite
fit this requirement, but no one has proved you can't use
them either! Getting distracted is an inevitable part of the
task, and happens to even the most experienced practitioners. The goal is to return your focus to your chosen object of
attention regardless of the distractions.

3. *Notice your thoughts.* Most likely, the main distraction will
be your own thoughts. Thoughts pop into our head hundreds of times in a day, so it is understandable that this will
happen during BMR too. When a thought pops in, notice it,
register it as a thought, then just focus back on the object of
your attention. This sounds easier than it is, because it is very

tempting to get involved in a thought, or get prompted to dwell on it, control it or do something because of it. For example, you may get the thought, 'I might be developing a cold.' Rather than worrying what would happen if you got a cold, just stop at that point. You have had a thought that you might be developing a cold. Notice that thought, and then go back to focusing your attention onto your breathing, or whatever you have chosen to focus on. The idea is to let the thought do its own thing. Some people even imagine their thought as a 'thought bubble' like in a cartoon, or imagine their thought floating past in a cloud. This might be helpful to you; everyone finds their own way of doing it.

4. *Let go of trying to control your thoughts.* So, we have established that thoughts pop into our heads lots of the time. We can't do anything about that. However, we can choose what we do afterwards, whether we follow that thought with a trail of other thoughts, ideas or worries; or whether we just notice the thought and focus back again on what we had been concentrating on. You are not trying to push the first thought to the back of your mind, or trying to eliminate it. You are just registering it, and letting the thought do its own thing, while you get on with doing your thing. The thought may well still be there, in the background of your mind, as you focus back on what you were doing. That's fine. Your thought will do what it does, and you will do what you want to do.

5. *Keep it manageable.* Accept that any attempt at BMR is a step in the right direction. There is no ideal time commitment for BMR. Practitioners of some similar techniques, like meditation, often seem to suggest that you need to carry them out for regular, sustained periods. However, BMR is not like that, as you decide how much and how often is useful to you. After all, it is not an end in itself. You have other things to do in your life! BMR is just a technique you

can carry out to explore what it is like to have a different kind of relationship with your thoughts.

This is just a brief introduction to BMR as another technique to try – a tool to add to your collection. At present, you may be willing to use it for some thoughts that you have, but not others. For your interest, appendix 3 provides some analogies that describe ways to face your thoughts and feelings that are similar to BMR. For example, some people are helped by seeing their thoughts in a train carriage that passes by them. In this way, they learn to realise that they are having the thought, but they don't need to be involved in it right now – 'I have a thought' rather than 'The thought has me'. By practising BMR, you can start to test whether it is OK to let go of trying to control your thoughts, and just let them be. What would happen if you did this? Do you need to control your thoughts immediately, or can you hold off just for a second or two and see what happens?

Stretching and relaxing muscles

You may have read about 'relaxation' as a treatment for anxiety, or tried it out yourself. In this book, I won't be suggesting that relaxation is a treatment for anxiety. You can do something much simpler.

When people feel anxious or panicky, one thing they often do is tense their muscles. Sometimes this is automatic and goes unnoticed. Some people do it because they think it will stop them from falling over if they feel unsteady on their feet. Other people may do it to prepare themselves to escape or to try to distract themselves from the feeling of anxiety. The problem is that when people tense their muscles for a long time, they actually feel more anxious, not less. You could try it now. You could try tensing your fists and arm muscles. When I do it, I feel more stressed, not less, and that is generally what other people report. So, what this means is that sometimes people will start tensing their muscles when they are facing something stressful. Then, they feel even more tense, not because of the situation but because of their own tendency to tense up. Some people may do other things, like fidgeting or moving around quickly. Each of these behaviours make the person doing them feel more anxious. The person doing these things thinks it's the situation making them anxious. However, in reality, part of it is what they are doing themselves. By practising stretching and relaxing your muscles, you can start to test any beliefs you might have that you would collapse or lose control if you were to stop tensing up when you feel anxious. Relax them and see what happens.

So what can you do? It is similar to the points for hyperventilation:

1. *Notice that you are tensing your muscles or moving around quickly.* Again, this is the most important stage, and not easy for anyone. Often your attention is on your worries and not on your body. So, when you are worrying, try to focus on your body. You could try scanning it from head to toe. Am I tensing my muscles in my neck, my arms, my hands, my legs? If you are, then gradually focus on this tension in a calm and slow manner. Be aware of what is going on in your body, and in your own time, move onto the next stage. If you are not tensing, then that's OK. Maybe muscle tension is not making the anxiety worse. It could be hyperventilation (see earlier). Or it could be your thoughts.
2. *Stretch and relax.* Focus on the part of your body that is tense. Stretch it and then relax it. Let the tension go. You may need to do this a couple of times but probably no more.
3. *Return to what you are doing.* When you have allowed the tension to go from your muscles, it is important to return to

what you were doing. Relaxation is a coping strategy rather than a treatment. Doing it lots will not make you even better – but it does help you get out of that vicious cycle of reacting to anxiety with tension which then makes you more anxious. Now try to focus back again on your surroundings and what you are doing.

You may be starting to see a pattern here. The techniques in this book are not treatments in themselves. They are ways to begin to step out of cycles of anxiety, behaviour and thinking that people get into. The good thing is that, with time, people learn to step out of these cycles more automatically, or not even to get into them in the first place. Then the technique is not needed for a while. So these techniques are not a one-off magic cure. Neither are they regularly enforced rituals. They are tools for you to use when you need them. Like any toolbox, you keep it in storage to use when you need it, but for the rest of the time you do other things.

Experience of tensing and relaxing muscles – Laura

> I found it immensely useful to know after all this time that we can, by being anxious and tensing our muscles and hyperventilating, create additional internal stress which isn't a direct result of the external stress. We can end up 're-infecting' ourselves by doing things that add to the problem rather than help it. I did always wonder about this and now I have an answer that seems to fit.

Taking a step back

This is another very simple coping strategy. It is like a very brief version of BMR. Some of our most problematic times occur when we are caught up in our thoughts, maybe thinking about the past or the future, rather than noticing what is going on

right now. 'Taking a step back' is about catching this, and stepping outside these thoughts for just a moment. It's about
putting a delay between your experience and how you react
to it. 'What is really going on right now?' is another way of
describing this technique. I have found it interesting how many
of my clients have spontaneously described starting to do this
more, after their therapy has finished. It may work on the basis
that you'll get a much better idea of how to cope with a situation
by noticing what is actually going on at the time, than you will
from delving into your mind for answers. Your mind just contains memories from the past and ideas about the future that
may or may not turn out to be correct. Yet the 'present' contains real information about what is happening, and how to
deal with the situation effectively.

Helpful things to remember

When you get an insight, or a new way of seeing your experiences, it can be helpful to note it down. This technique is a bit
like using proverbs or quotes like the ones peppered throughout this book. You are very likely to have your own, very individual, learning experiences that are most helpful for you. Not
that you want to litter your house with proverbs and sparky
insights in every visible space, but you might save the best ones
to put somewhere that you can return to when you feel they
may be of help.

Drawing on strengths, qualities and resources

This point is really a general way of thinking about all of the
points above. They are ways of thinking or acting that you are
adding to your 'mental toolbox'. You will have many more that
you will develop or rediscover. You may be creative, or be good
at doing tasks that other people find difficult, or you may have

the resource of friends and acquaintances with ideas that could be helpful. The principle is that a fear, a phobia, or another problematic situation is a difficulty that you are preparing for, using the strengths and resources that you have. Sometimes it may feel that these strengths and qualities are no longer there, for example when you are tired, low or exhausted. This is natural. Our mood has a big effect on how well we can remember our good qualities. As people begin to cope, they tend to accept that sometimes they are not aware of all their strengths all of the time. Their strengths are still there, and they become aware of them again at other times, and they build them up over time. Chapter 11 includes more information about strengths, values and resources.

Self-soothing

Many of us get into struggles in our heads where we criticise ourselves for not coping, or for making mistakes. An alternative way of talking to ourselves is to say things that are accepting of our distress and any mistakes we may make, and provide hope and possible ideas for how to cope in the future. In fact, there is evidence that this self-soothing approach has an effect on the chemicals in the brain that provide natural release from pain – the endorphins. These studies have been reviewed by the therapist and researcher Paul Gilbert, and inform the way he uses cognitive therapy. Here are some examples of statements that reflect this idea. Of course, while it may help to say these, the real benefit will come when you start to believe them, maybe when you have seen evidence that they can help you to cope.

Everyone gets distressed at times. It is normal to be upset, anxious or angry.

I know that my distress is real because I can feel it in my body.

My distress is completely appropriate given my past experiences, and what I believe might be happening now or in the future.

My feelings of distress will eventually drop with time. I know this because it has happened before, but I understand that it is hard for me to accept this right now.

When I feel very low it is difficult to think of my strengths, qualities and worth as a human being, but I understand that they are still there, to be rediscovered and built on in the future.

If I cope with a situation just as well as before and no better, that is a good step.

If I learn to cope with a situation even slightly better than before, that is also a good step.

I realise that I will have setbacks. This is a normal part of learning to cope.

Everyone makes mistakes. It is one way that we learn to cope in the future.

Diet

There is one more area to consider, that I have left to the end of this chapter because it is less to do with psychology than the others, but no less important. There is evidence that diet has an effect on our ability to think, reason and manage our emotions. This is not that surprising given that what we eat builds and keeps our brain and body working well. Getting a balanced diet of protein (for essential amino acids), fat (for lining the tubes that send signals between brain cells), fruit and vegetables (for most important vitamins) would seem the most appropriate choice, and there are other books that explain what this would involve. You may also consider trying vitamin and mineral supplements if your diet is not balanced for any reason. Also, the evidence that omega-3 can help mental health is persuasive, so you may consider eating more oily fish, or taking cod liver oil tablets. Drinking more than four or five caffeinated drinks per day (tea, coffee, cola, energy drinks), can increase the physical effects of anxiety, so you may consider trying to reduce your caffeine intake. None of these suggestions would eliminate a person's anxiety, as diet is rarely the main cause, but they may well increase a person's ability to learn to cope better.

Key points

- Just a little practice of coping strategies can be helpful.
- Hyperventilation, or over-breathing, is harmless.
- People can learn to slow down their breathing to a normal rate.
- Thoughts pop into our heads hundreds of times in a day.
- After a thought has popped into our heads, we can choose what to do or think.
- It can be helpful to 'take a step back' and see what is going on right now, in the present.
- People's awareness of their strengths comes and goes with changes in their mood, even though their strengths are still there.

4

Understanding fear

Normal fear protects us; abnormal fear paralyses us. Normal fear motivates us to improve our individual and collective welfare; abnormal fear constantly poisons and distorts our inner lives. Our problem is not to be rid of fear but, rather to harness and master it.

Martin Luther King Jr

Acceptance of what has happened is the first step to overcoming the consequences of any misfortune.

William James

Fear can be helpful!

In this section, I explain why fear is not only normal but actually an inevitable part of being human and a vital way to keep safe from real danger. It is clear that when we are anxious, our body is reacting differently from usual. All the bodily changes that people feel when they are anxious are part of the way that our body prepares to face a real danger. For many kinds of danger, these reactions are extremely useful, so they indicate that your body is actually working as it should. Hopefully, this will become clearer once the fear reaction is explained in detail.

Three stages to fear

There are three stages to fear: Detection, Interpretation and Response. All three stages are present in all animals and humans, whether they have phobias or not.

Detection

First, some kind of change is detected. This change can be literally anything. It can be in the world outside, or it can be in your own mind or body. It could be the crack of a twig behind you, a memory that pops into your head, a thought about what other people might be saying, or a pain. When a person notices a change, their attention is drawn towards it. Sometimes it can feel as if the change 'captures' or 'possesses' your attention, which can be a very distressing feeling in itself.

Obviously, the bigger the change, the more it will attract a person's attention. Loud noises and sudden movements have a powerful ability to grab attention. Vivid memories, unusual thoughts and intense feelings in our bodies also have this capacity. It certainly makes sense to notice these things, as they could well be important. Everyone is 'hard-wired' to do this, because it is vitally important that we notice changes around us. And the more pronounced the change, the more important it is to notice it, although some people are more sensitive to this than others. However, at this stage it is not absolutely certain that the change indicates a danger; it could be something quite harmless. This comes in the second stage.

Interpretation

After a person notices a change, he or she focuses on it, to see what it means. This stage can occur very quickly. So, say for example you are walking in a local wood and you hear a twig break behind you. What is your first thought? This scenario sounds like it could be threatening. Your immediate reaction could well be fear – this interpretation occurs in an instant. However, what if I were to give you more information about the situation? You are actually walking with a friend who is a few paces behind you. Now it seems obvious that the sound of a twig breaking is not a sign of danger at all. It is just your friend walking behind you. This stage is very important because it helps us to distinguish something that is a real danger from something that is a false alarm. A false alarm is something we can ignore, and so get back to what we were doing before we were interrupted. This example demonstrates that often it is not what we see or hear that is a danger, but how we explain it to ourselves that counts. Often, when we take time to take in more of the situation around us (for example, 'a friend is behind me'), then that thing we notice becomes much less threatening.

You might suggest that this is all very well, but some things are just inherently dangerous. A fierce tiger, for example. Surely that is dangerous whatever the situation? Yet a bit of imagination shows that this is not the case either. What if the tiger is in a secure cage? What if it is a perfect holographic projection of a fierce tiger that you know is not real? Again the way you understand the situation dictates whether this thing is dangerous or not.

There are many research studies which show that people with phobias are more likely than other people to come up with a threatening explanation for these kind of scenarios, and they seem to do this quite automatically. Part of learning to cope with phobias is noticing this tendency, and to take in more information, to see whether the threat might be less than you had initially imagined. There might be things that you had overlooked. For example, if you are talking to a group of people, it may initially seem that one of them is scowling at you. However, when you look again you see that they are actually leaning forward to try to concentrate on what you are saying. When people with phobias do take in more information, they can change their mind and realise that the situation is not as dangerous as they had originally thought. This shows that people with phobias are not in any way irrational – they can generate a more helpful and realistic explanation of a situation when they are able to consider different alternatives. The difference is that, for people with phobias, the more threatening explanation seems to come to mind first, and then they tend to stick to this explanation and react with fear, rather than looking for more information that might reassure them that a situation is actually safe.

So, fear happens suddenly and can be quite intense. Yet when the person tries to react as quickly as possible to something dangerous, this seems to get in the way of really checking the situation out. Of course, sometimes there just isn't time to do this, and anyone would have to react in the same way. But ideally, we would face a fearful situation slowly, giving ourselves time to consider non-threatening explanations and assess what danger is really there. Appendix 1 gives some examples of non-threatening interpretations for some common experiences.

Response

Once a person (or animal) has interpreted a change as a likely danger, this triggers a bodily reaction to prepare for escape. This whole process can happen in less than a second. For example, we jump and get startled when someone creeps up behind us and shouts 'Boo!' This is a helpful response – it alerts us to a possible danger. One really vivid example is to imagine a gazelle on the savannah of Africa. The gazelle is feeding quietly, when it detects a movement in the grass. It identifies the movement as a lion, so it reacts instantly by racing away. It escapes to safety. Clearly this is a vital response. If the gazelle had left it any longer, it may have been caught and eaten. The gazelle's likelihood of escape is made even greater by the way that its fear has led to changes in its body that prepare it for a fast escape. The way that the body does this efficiently is for one chemical circulating in our blood to have effects on many different parts of the body. That chemical is adrenaline. The same process occurs in humans, in all kinds of situations. The threat may also be a threat from an animal like a spider or snake, or the threat could come from a person or even a change in your own body or mind (for example, a scary thought). In each case, a human will experience a surge of adrenaline in the same way as a gazelle.

The effects of adrenaline on the body are widespread. For the gazelle, this is a godsend. It breathes faster so that it gets more oxygen into the body to give it vital energy. Its heart beats

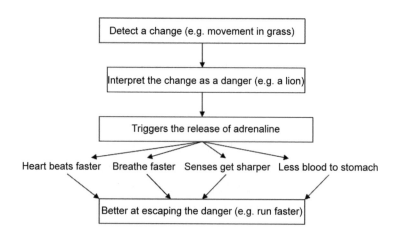

more quickly, pumping the oxygen to the muscles in its legs as it races away to safety. Blood is also diverted away from parts of the body that are less important at that moment during escape, such as the stomach, so that more oxygen can be directed to the muscles. Adrenaline also affects the senses, making them sharper and more acute, so the gazelle can spot an ideal escape route and find safety. All of these bodily reactions are helping the gazelle to escape. They are vital to its survival.

What does this mean about feelings of fear?

Hopefully you agree with the above explanation, but you may not at the moment, which is fine for now – or there may just be certain bits that you can sort out later. However, understanding fear in the way I have described, does have some interesting implications. It means that fear is normal. It is an inevitable consequence of life – we will often notice things that might be dangerous. Fear, and its effects on our body are helpful in certain situations. Our feelings of anxiety are important because they are a warning of possible danger. They suggest to us that something is afoot – but the way to really work out if there is a danger is to check it out. Look for more information. See if there are reasons to feel in danger, or reasons to feel safe. Taking more information in, rather than relying just on our feelings, seems to be the way to do this. Feelings are just a hint, sometimes accurate, sometimes misleading. The real information about danger is around you.

The close relationship between mind and body

An important message from what we have covered so far, is that the mind and the body are closely linked. What we think affects how our body responds (for example, the thought of being in danger triggers the release of adrenaline), and when we notice our body's response this leads us to think certain things (for example, when we feel short of breath we may think we are in danger of suffocating). It is not too difficult now to see how these can lead to a vicious cycle, where the fear of suffocating leads to a further rush of adrenaline which in turn makes the bodily sensations more intense, leading to the thought that we must be in real danger, and so increasing the fear and keeping the cycle going. Later on, we will plot out these vicious cycles, and show how it is possible to step outside the cycles by thinking about your experiences in different ways – thoughts that are not the same threatening ideas that you may have at the moment.

There is also a nice positive consequence of the close link between mind and body. It means we can create cycles that are helpful to us, 'virtuous cycles' that build us up both mentally and physically. One example is thinking about being understood in a compassionate way. Imagine yourself talking to a considerate person who listens to what you have been through. Talking to a person in this way triggers brain chemicals that have beneficial effects on your body (they are called endorphins or natural opiates) and it is these chemicals that naturally soothe emotional and physical pain. The cognitive therapist Paul Gilbert has worked intensively on studying the role of these kinds of brain systems in therapy – his work has more information on the scientific explanation of this process if you are interested. The self-soothing ways of thinking to yourself described at the end of the last chapter may have similar positive effects. Like all the ideas in this book, it is not the one, single solution to anxiety problems, but it can help some people.

What kinds of things do people fear?

It seems that there is almost no limit to the different kinds of things of which people can be afraid. People are often more familiar with the phobias of things in the outside world like heights, injections, certain animals, natural phenomena such as lightning and flood, and objects such as bridges and balloons. Some fears are much broader, such as being scrutinised or judged by other people, or going too far from home. People often fear experiences in their own bodies or minds, such as sensations of breathlessness; emotions such as sadness, anger or disgust that a person finds unacceptable; thoughts or images of germs all over their hands that compel them to clean themselves; and memories of past traumatic experiences that people try to push out of their mind. This means that even if the things that you are afraid of seem unusual to other people, there is no reason to believe your fears are abnormal. The range is very broad. People fear very different things from one another because we all have unique experiences and make our own judgements about what is dangerous. Appendix 1 provides a range of other examples.

As there are so many things that people fear, it might seem that a different treatment is needed for each one, making it very complicated. However, this is not the case for two reasons. First, because, whatever the source of the phobia, the same principles that we have covered seem to apply. For example, in all phobias, people tend to be particularly sensitive to noticing the things of which they are afraid. Second, there is one source of fear that is the same across all these phobias, namely the bodily feelings of fear itself. This is why learning to face, understand and tolerate these feelings in our own bodies is such a useful part of coping. Often it is not the thing itself (for example, a spider) that we are afraid of, but of the way that it makes us feel (for example, disgusted or frightened), and what we think these feelings mean. For example, one client interpreted her feelings when she saw a spider as signalling 'the presence of evil'. We discussed how these feelings might be better explained as her normal fear reaction triggered by adrenaline. We discussed whether the spider was evil or not, and how could you tell? If the spider had the spirit of a saint but still looked like a spider, moved like a spider, and made her feel nervous, then would it still be 'evil'? We shall return several times to learning to tolerate feelings of anxiety a small step at a time.

Examples of Alice's different fears

> I was very afraid of driving to my local large town to go shopping. There seemed to be several things that I feared. I could not face having to stop at traffic lights, driving along a red route because I could not stop if I wanted to, being surrounded by heavy traffic, driving up the High Street, parking the car and leaving the car. Just the thought of doing any of these things caused me to feel anxious, especially my heart beating fast and a feeling of unreality. To me the town represented a dangerous jungle.

Rasheeda's experience of facing the feelings of anxiety

> One thing that held me back at first was the belief that I was far too afraid and anxious when it came to the object of my phobia, spiders, to ever be cured. I was aware that the process of recovery would require me sometimes to do things, for example, be quite near a spider or watch it while it moves, that made me feel intensely anxious and I wasn't quite sure I would be able to pull through. I learnt however that the intense feeling of anxiety doesn't last very long, and instead of getting worse the longer I persist, the better it gets until I actually stop feeling anxious. So, for example, when looking at a spider move, if I keep looking at it instead of averting my eyes to look somewhere else, the anxiety I am feeling will in fact lessen anyway until it disappears even though I am still watching the spider.

How do fears begin?

There is no single answer to what causes fears and phobias. Problems with anxiety do tend to run in families. Research indicates that part of the cause is inherited and part is caused by what happens to us early on in life. These studies are carried out in several ways. One kind of study takes advantage of the fact that identical twins have identical genes. We get our genes from our parents. They are fixed before we are born and do not change during our lifetime, whatever happens to us. The most informative studies are ones where two identical twins have been adopted and are reared apart. In this way, they only share the same genes and not the same environment. It is found that if one twin has an anxiety disorder then there is a much greater chance that the other twin will have anxiety disorder too. This means that genes do affect whether a person gets an anxiety disorder. However, genes are not even half of the story. There is a large proportion of identical twins for whom only one of the pair has an anxiety disorder (or any kind of phobia). This must mean that people's experiences are important too.

There is a great deal of evidence that certain fears develop naturally at a certain age during childhood in most children. For example, the fear of heights appears around the age of eighteen to twenty-four months when a child is mobile and therefore risks falling over. So what leads these fears to become phobias in adulthood for some people? Although the evidence is in its early stages, it seems that it depends on the way that the caregivers of the child (usually the parents) deal with the fear and the child's distress about it. Some parents will comfort their child, listen to their concerns and help them to face this situation in future. These children tend to lose their fears with time. Other parents, however, may be convinced that there was a real danger and respond to the child's distress by trying to prevent any slightly risky situations of the same kind in future. They may also sometimes be very critical of their child's anxiety problems, rather than accepting them and helping them learn how to deal with them. These children are more likely to develop phobias. For more information in this area, you may be interested in reading another book in this series by Sam Cartwright-Hatton which is in the reading list at the back of this book.

It is important to note that phobias are not simply caused by genes and parenting style. Some people may have distressing experiences that trigger the phobia, or make it worse. Sometimes these experiences may be severe traumatic events such as serious injury, prolonged bullying, sexual assault or witnessing violence or death at close hand. Indeed, there is one disorder, post-traumatic stress disorder (PTSD), that is partly defined by the past experience of a trauma. Other anxiety problems can be triggered by traumas too. Some people who have experienced or witnessed a trauma, such as a car accident, may engage in repetitive checking. For example, they may check their car repeatedly after driving past a pedestrian, just in case they might have been responsible for an accident too.

Other people report frightening experiences that are less traumatic, but nonetheless personally powerful, such as being lost in a supermarket, or being stranded in a thunderstorm. So, at the very least, we need to consider that genes, parenting behaviour and personal experiences contribute to phobias. The balance of which of these is more important will vary widely between different people, and these experiences build upon one another over a person's life.

When these experiences occur early on in life, they are more likely to have a big effect on a person's way of thinking. Psychological therapy can help people to see how these ways of thinking started, which often involves talking about distressing experiences from the past and being heard in a considerate way. The therapy also often helps people to see how their past experiences have coloured their thinking in the present. Often there is a close relationship between the past experience and the current problem. For example, it is common for people with fears of physical illnesses to have close family members who have died from the illness they are worried about. People with fears of social situations have often experienced nasty incidents of bullying or teasing at a young age. People with claustrophobic fears have often had frightening experiences of being smothered or restrained in some way. In my experience, it seems as though these experiences build up over a person's life, and at each stage they make decisions to try to prevent the bad experiences from happening again in a way that gears their life in a certain direction. Part of learning to cope is gradually realising the way that your life has been directed by events like this, and trying out a new direction where instead of trying to avoid the danger, you try to face it. Is this current situation really the same as it was in the past? How could I respond differently to what is happening right now that is different from how I managed then?

Making these links does not have to occur in therapy itself, but it seems as though a safe relationship with another person is important. In this book, I can't create a real relationship with you, the reader, but I do hope that reading the book will allow you to think about what kind of real relationship you might want to find that helps you to talk about these experiences. Again, this is probably not the complete answer but is one of the things that others with phobias have found helpful.

Rasheeda's own explanation of how her phobia may have developed

As far as I remember, when I was really young I was not particularly afraid of spiders. One summer when I was eight or nine years old, I was sitting in a chair in the countryside absorbed in a book, legs dangling to the ground. At first I thought what was tickling my leg was a patch of grass, so instead of looking I just shifted my leg a bit to the side. After a few more attempts to get away from the patch of grass I looked down and saw a very large spider crawling up my leg. I kicked my leg to get rid of it while screaming really loudly. My mother ran to see what was going on and caught a

Continued

glimpse of the spider scampering away. She said it was really big and she tried to catch it with a saucepan but failed. It is quite possible that by trying to capture it she confirmed my fear that it was a dangerous creature. From then on whichever I saw a spider I asked my mother to remove it. She often tried to encourage me to do it myself or to do it together but I always refused, and in the end she always did it for me. I was really scared and she was only trying to help. However I never really learnt how to deal with a spider by myself.

As a teenager my fear of spiders wasn't a big problem in my everyday life. I grew up on the fourth floor of an apartment building in Istanbul so there weren't really many spiders around. It wasn't therefore something that I thought about very much. However, when I moved to the UK to go to university the house I lived in was old, with old plumbing, old floorboards and plenty of spiders. Going from seeing only a few spiders in the course of years, to finding at least one or two rather large ones every week was a great shock for me and I believe that is the time when my fear of spiders became full blown 'arachnophobia'.

Alice's own explanation of how her phobia may have developed

On consideration, I feel that the causes of my agoraphobia are genetic, environmental and from my parents' care of me. I was a very much wanted child of older parents. My mother was a very anxious person and suffered from claustrophobia and some agoraphobia. I was not allowed to do ordinary childhood adventurous activities like climbing trees. My mother's constant response was, 'Be careful!' or, 'You'll hurt yourself!' I do not blame my mother for this because she was a victim of her own anxieties. When I grew up I increasingly found my new environment threatening until I only really felt safe in my new home, I suppose because I had not learnt from my parents how to cope with unfamiliar places.

Memories and pictures in the mind

I have already underlined that we need to consider phobias of experiences in the mind and body as well as events that lie outside in the real world. I have talked already about the causes of the physical feelings in our body that come with anxiety. Also important are the memories and mental images that we get in our mind. Very often, when a person is confronted with the object of their fears (such as fur), they don't so much react to the object itself (for example, a furry toy), but to the images, and sometimes memories, that this object triggers in their mind. Many of these images are visual, but they can also involve sounds, smells and physical feelings – for this reason, they are sometimes called body memories. For example, a person who is afraid of fur may experience the mental image of being smothered by fur – this is clearly more frightening than a cuddly toy and explains why the person's anxiety is so extreme. Any of us would become anxious if we experienced being smothered by fur. What people see from the outside when a person with a phobia is reacting to an object, very rarely reflects what that person is really experiencing, inside their body and their mind.

So what is the cause of these mental images? Are they normal? There is a long history of psychological research into mental imagery. People can use mental images to navigate their way round new towns after memorising a map. They use it for solving spatial puzzles such as jigsaws. Our memory of the past is based partly on images stored in our minds that we somehow conjure up when we need to remember events. Mental imagery is not only normal but very important. The problem is when some of these images contain elements of which we are afraid. When these images from the past, which can feel very vivid and real, come back in the present, our tendency is to push them to the back of our minds rather than to really see them and manipulate them as you might do if it was the memory of the map of your town. Yet you can no more erase a distressing memory than you can force yourself to forget the layout of your local shopping centre. Pushing images to the back of our minds is an attempt to fool ourselves into thinking that they are not there, rather like believing you can avoid having to pay a parking fine by hiding it at the bottom of a drawer. You would be less aware of it there, but it would still exist. It seems that our memories cannot be erased in this way. However, psychologists have found that if people experience these images, and notice how they may often be memories of past events, they can start to piece together a story of how they developed their fears. When people have a clear understanding of these past incidents and have started to confront them, the images start to have less of an impact on them in the present.

An example of an image that Alice experiences

I once had to wait almost two hours for a bus home from town. I had panic attacks while I was waiting. Since that time, over thirty years ago, I have not travelled on a bus. The image of that long wait and myself panicking comes back into my mind when I am in similar situations.

Rasheeda's images of spiders

During my phobia I often had vivid images of spiders in my head. This was quite disrupting as the images would cause me intense anxiety, often equivalent to the anxiety I felt when I was actually encountering a spider. Following the image popping up in my mind I would often feel like there were spiders on me, which caused me even more anxiety. Images would most often 'haunt' me at night time when I was trying to sleep. When at its worst this intrusive imagery disturbed me in my sleep which affected me during the day quite a lot as I was constantly tired. The way I tried to cope with these images was by trying to banish them from my

Continued

mind. Either by thinking about something else, or turning on the light and keeping my eyes open, sometimes I even tried pinching myself for distraction. None of these techniques must have been working as the intrusive imagery persisted up until I had therapy. During the therapy, I discovered that some of the images I had were very similar to experiences I had with spiders as a child. It was as though my brain had remembered those times, even though I had not deliberately thought about them.

The signs are that people who learn to face, focus on and piece together the scary images in their mind, can learn to cope with their fears better. This seems to be for two reasons. First, if these memories are of real events, then by being aware of them people actually get a better understanding of their past and how they got to where they are. Second, when looking at memories and images in this way, people begin to see them as what they are – images and memories, rather than the distressing events happening all over again. It's rather like editing the clips from a frightening movie. When we watch a horror film in a darkened cinema, the scary scenes can often jump out of the blue and make us want to turn away. However, imagine you were to get hold of the movie reel, or get an electronic version to manipulate on a computer. You can now see the scenes that make up the movie. You could slow them down, speed them up, maybe even change the order or the ending. Now it's a lot easier to look at those scenes and see them as bits of film, rather than the event itself, while at the same time understanding the movie in more detail.

Another way of thinking about a mental image is to see it as the map of a location. If you were using a map to plan a difficult, stressful journey, you wouldn't be afraid of the piece of paper with the map on it. In the same way, an image in our head is like a map of the outside world. The outside world can help us or harm us, but the image cannot do this. It can only prepare us for what we plan to do.

How Rasheeda learnt to cope with her images

Anything small that tickles me, like a piece of string that's hanging from my clothing immediately makes me think of spiders and makes me nervous. I get the physical feeling of spiders crawling on me and I feel tickly all over. This I am sure stems from my first encounter with a large spider, where initially I had mistaken the tickling on my leg as a piece of grass and ignored it thus letting the spider crawl almost up to my knee. Before therapy I used to fidget a lot as I was trying to calm the sensation of being tickled, and I suppose subconsciously I was also checking that the feeling wasn't indeed coming from a real spider. Since therapy I have learnt to stay with the moment and let the feeling fade on its own. As a result the experience of it doesn't last as long as it used to.

Since I have had my therapy and have made considerable recovery from my phobia, these intrusive images have mostly disappeared. I still get the odd dream of spiders, but the anxiety this causes me is much less intense than it used to be, sometimes I don't even wake up. And if I do get an intrusive image I now know how to cope with it. I have learnt that suppressing these images is not helpful. If I just let the image play in my mind for a little while then it will invariably go away on its own, as the anxiety it has caused fades away too.

Again, take your time with each of these techniques. There is no rush to relive all of your childhood experiences, or focus on mental images at the expense of everyday life. You have your own ways of doing things that may well have served you OK up until now. Trying new things out will come a bit at a time, and even then, only if you want to. So, I will be returning to this topic a little later.

When is avoiding danger a good way of coping?

You may be picking up the message, either from this book, or from other sources, that avoiding what you are afraid of is bad: 'avoidance is bad'. I would hope that by the end of this book, you don't think of it in quite that way.

Avoiding danger is not bad in a moral way – it is not really something that someone should feel guilty about because it has a very understandable purpose. Avoiding what you are afraid of can be very helpful. For example, it is very dangerous to stand at the edge of a cliff without any safety equipment. So, avoiding the edge of a cliff is not only helpful, but could be life-saving. We all have an in-built tendency to avoid what we fear. The same probably applies for experiences in our own minds and bodies too. It is probably a good idea to avoid experiences that seem extremely threatening, because facing an experience like that would be overwhelming for anyone. This is why learning to face fears is done a little bit at a time. Learning to face fears will not take away your ability to avoid a situation when you really need to.

So when is avoidance not an appropriate way to deal with danger? The answer to this is a bit vague, and may become clearer as you read further. In essence, avoidance seems to be unhelpful when a person avoids an experience in their mind or body because they believe that the experience in itself will lead to a terrible and real catastrophe. In other words, they are treating the feeling, thought, or memory, as the real danger, rather than as a feeling, thought or memory *of* the danger. They are treating things in their own heads and bodies as though they were real events in the world. Hopefully, part of what you will be doing while working through this book is separating the thoughts from the reality, learning to tolerate the thoughts or feelings about dangerous events, without having to actually confront the real danger at all!

Avoiding danger – Paul

For many years I changed what I did to try to cope with my anxiety. I would not go into places where there were groups of lads, because I was convinced they would attack me. I would sometimes just have to rush home because it seemed too dangerous to go onto the streets. I was really worried about looking weak, so I wore clothes to make me look bigger. I tried not to look other men in the eyes. For a long time I felt that I had to do these things to stay safe, and I do live in a bad area of London where there are attacks every week. So I think they helped me in a way. But I did know that I had to try to cope too and that these things I was doing were making my life very difficult – I couldn't even go to the local shops unless it was really quiet.

Key points

- Fear can be a vital way to keep safe from real danger.
- Feelings of anxiety can be caused by the release of adrenaline in the body.
- Fear can be triggered by things in the outside world and also by mental events like thoughts and images.
- Some people learn to be less afraid of the pictures they have in their mind when they realise that some of them are memories.
- Avoiding danger is one way of trying to cope.

5

Understanding vicious cycles and how to step outside them

Whatever we expect with confidence becomes our own self-fulfilling prophecy.

Brian Tracy

The quest for certainty blocks the search for meaning. Uncertainty is the very condition to impel man to unfold his powers.

Erich Fromm

Vicious cycles

It can be difficult to understand why fear is such a big problem for some people and not for others. Are some people just different? Or have more bad things happened to them? These are both possible, but how we try to deal with our problems can also make them worse. Sometimes the very ways that we try to control our fears can keep the fears going or even escalate them. This is a 'vicious cycle', which I will explain in more detail in this chapter. The cycle is made up of several different parts. I will explain each of these in turn.

Anxiety provoking situations

For most of us, there are situations in which we feel relatively safe, and situations in which we feel in danger. For example, a person with agoraphobia may feel comfortable at home with a close family member, but anxious when left alone in a supermarket. The first stage in forming a vicious cycle is the situation itself – where you are, and what is going on around you. Each person will have different kinds of situations that make them anxious.

```
┌─────────────────────────────┐
│                             │
│          Situation          │
│                             │
└─────────────────────────────┘
```

Physical sensations and mental events that are triggered in the situation or appear out of the blue

The next stage is something that is triggered inside your body or your mind. This experience can be a thought that pops into your mind, an image that appears, a sudden physical sensation, or a change in mood. Psychologists have shown that these kinds of experiences can be 'automatic', that is they can occur suddenly, and are not caused deliberately. So for example, sometimes people wake up with their heart racing but there seems to be no obvious cause. Or they may experience a sudden pain. Another example would be getting a thought that is out of character for you, like: 'I could hit that person!'

If these unusual sensations or mental events were to suddenly appear, especially during your first few panic attacks, and felt so severe that you really believed that something terrible was about to happen, then it is very understandable that you would be overwhelmingly worried and think the worst. People who experience this are often then on the look out for more signs – they show 'selective attention' to certain experiences. Selective attention is basically what we focus on – what we look at, listen to and feel at any one time, out of everything around us. For example, if you were at a zoo, you might decide to find the penguins because you like them, hunt them out using the map and spend time watching their antics when you find them. You only have a day ticket and it's a big zoo so you would miss seeing many of the other animals that you are less interested in. In other words, people only take in a tiny amount of what is around them. Interestingly, much of this is their own thoughts and feelings rather than what is in their surroundings.

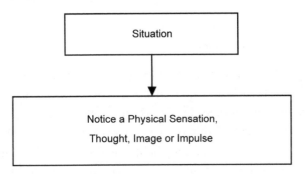

Some people have more extreme threatening beliefs about these experiences

Focusing on unusual bodily sensations and mental events is not a problem in itself. However, some people start to come up with catastrophic ideas about what these experiences might mean. If these ideas are extreme, it doesn't mean that the ideas are definitely not true. For example, someone feeling their heart race suddenly may be convinced that they are about to have a heart attack and collapse at any moment. It is understandable to have this catastrophic thought about such an unusual sensation. Now, it may or may not be true that this person is about to have a heart attack – this is just one possibility. However, if the person is convinced, they may not even consider other possibilities, for example, that this is a normal increase in heart rate that comes with increased fear or after exercise.

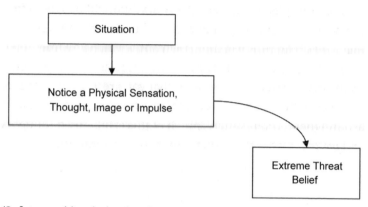

'Safety-seeking behaviour'

Doing something to make yourself feel safe is an understandable reaction to having an experience that you believe is extremely threatening or frightening. The things that people do to try to escape from the bad things they are worried might happen to them are called 'safety-seeking behaviour', or 'safety behaviours' for short, a term coined by the cognitive therapist, Paul Salkovskis. The person doing these things believes that doing them makes them safe, but doing them makes the person more convinced that the catastrophe would have happened if they hadn't prevented it themselves with their saftey behaviours. For example, a man who notices his heart racing and is convinced he is about to have a heart attack may sit down as quickly as possible, 'Thank God I sat down in time, otherwise I might have had a heart attack!' he thinks to himself, 'I've had a near miss!' So, safety behaviours prevent a person from really testing out their fears. In this example, just sitting down cannot avert an imminent heart attack. But, when the person does sit down and their attention goes away from their heart, they start to believe that a heart attack has been averted. They still believe they have a weak heart because they have not just continued what they were doing and let their heart rate drop by itself. Sometimes, outside the situation, it all seems quite different. The anxious person may say,

'You know, I didn't really believe that I was having a heart attack.' It can seem odd to have believed in this extreme catastrophe when thinking about it afterwards. This provides a great opportunity though; next time, the person can try to drop the safety behaviour and test what actually does happen.

There are many examples of safety behaviours. They include avoiding distressing situations, escaping from them, pushing distressing thoughts out of one's mind, repetitive rituals like checking, cleaning or hoarding, and exaggerated attempts to control one's weight or body shape. For some people, even the constructive things they do can be driven by fear – like working extremely hard to prove oneself to others or to avoid failure. What marks what we do as a safety behaviour is if the person does it to try to stop something from happening that they believe will be catastrophic. Safety behaviours typically do not make the person more safe, although they may feel more safe or believe that the behaviours are working. It is worth noting that everyday behaviours that avert real danger are not safety behaviours in the same sense – like looking both ways before crossing the road or wearing warm clothes in winter. These typically avert real threat, and do not have the negative effects that safety behaviours have, which are covered below.

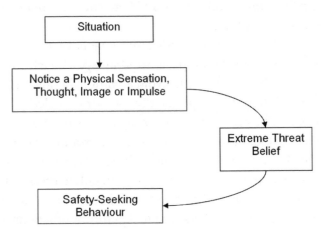

Completing the cycle: the effects of safety-seeking behaviours

There are at least three ways that using a safety behaviour feeds into a vicious cycle to keep it going:

1. *They confirm the threat belief.* I mentioned this one above – by engaging in the safety behaviour, the person becomes convinced that it was their action (their safety behaviour) that averted a catastrophe, or reduced how severe it was. Only by dropping the safety behaviour and enduring the situation without it, can they discover that the situation would not turn out in the extremely threatening way that they had imagined.

2. *They lead to increases in unusual physical sensations and mental events.* For example, some people who are afraid of looking nervous in groups, use the safety behaviour of gripping their hands to try to stop them trembling – they think other people will ridicule or reject them if their hands are shaking. But, gripping their hands actually makes a person feel more tense and rigid, which leads to more worry about looking nervous. Another example is pushing distressing thoughts out of your mind. When people have studied this in the laboratory, it actually leads the thoughts to 'rebound' – they pop back into a person's head later. There are many other examples like this.

3. *They affect the situation itself and may have an impact on other people.* One example is avoiding eye contact, which is one way that people try to avoid attention, because they are worried about being 'put on the spot' or ridiculed by other people. The problem is that when you talk to a person who does not look at you, it disrupts the conversation. It may even lead the other person to think that someone who doesn't look at them is not interested in them. Often it seems that it is the safety behaviours themselves that can affect the way a person is seen by others, and makes future situations more

difficult. Indeed, when a person avoids any situation (for example, the dentist, work, meeting strangers, exercise) for a long period of time, it makes facing that situation more difficult because they are out of practice. When a person has avoided a situation for a long time, it is unrealistic to think that they can just face it again. Like any skill it takes practice, and needs to develop a step at a time.

The diagram below brings together all the parts of the vicious cycle and shows the three effects of safety behaviours as different arrows.

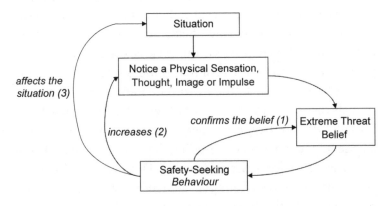

Vicious cycles are easy to fall into

Vicious cycles are a very common pattern to get into, but some of us fall into them more easily than others. It happens when all of the above start to occur together. The kinds of physical sensations and mental events in the second box are common, yet because they are experienced from 'within', we don't often talk about them. So they seem frightening and unknown. I have listed many of these in appendix 1 towards the end of the book, because many people are afraid of even reading too much about them. As they are at the back, you can read them in your own time. People often think these experiences are a sign of personal weakness, or serious physical or mental illness. They don't realise that they are very common because other people don't talk about them either. For example, there is a study that surveyed people without psychological problems and found that they experienced some of the same unusual thoughts as people with obsessive-compulsive disorder, yet they were less distressed and preoccupied by them. The reference for this study (Rachman & de Silva, 1978) can be found in the reading list in appendix 5.

Also, most people do not realise that these kinds of experiences disappear with time, once the person is feeling less stressed. Yet, because people think about these experiences in extreme ways, they try to get rid of them, suppress them or criticise themselves for having them, and this leads to more unpleasant experiences – a vicious cycle is formed. At a peak of panic, the vicious cycle can spiral round to the point that the person feels trapped in their own body and mind, feeling as though they want to escape from themselves and their fears. This is understandably a very distressing state, and one that has a huge impact on a person, leading them to remember it, and try to avoid it for years afterwards. However, by doing so, people try to avoid all feelings of anxiety, which is very difficult to maintain. In this book, we will try to see how a person can tolerate some feelings of anxiety, while stepping outside the cycle of increasing symptoms, so that they do not spiral downwards in a vicious cycle. The key is to notice your thoughts about those feelings, and how you respond to them.

Some examples of vicious cycles

The specific examples of vicious cycles in this section illustrate how it is possible for situations to become more anxiety-provoking over time, and for people to build up worrying beliefs about their physical sensations and mental events, including a range of safety behaviours, which they believe are saving them from catastrophe. The first example is a story rather than a real experience, which a well known cognitive therapist, Paul Salkovskis, often uses. It illustrates some of the main points behind Cognitive Behavioural Therapy (CBT).

A man inherits a beautiful mansion from a distant relative. The executor of the will tells him, 'There is a piece of string suspended from the ceiling on the top floor of the house. On no account should you ever pull this string!' The man is very concerned so he makes sure that the door to this room is locked at all times. However, this doesn't stop him thinking, 'But what if someone breaks down the door and pulls the string?' So he decides to put a barricade around his house just to make sure. Unfortunately, this still doesn't stop him thinking what might happen if some desperate person were to climb the barricades and barge their way into the house. So, he employs several stern-looking guards to patrol the perimeter – but he still can't be absolutely sure that the string will stay intact. So he checks the string every hour, day and night. By this time, his life has become extremely restricted and he becomes desperate and he has nothing left to lose. He goes up to the locked room. He tentatively opens the door. He looks at the string from the door. Could this really be so dangerous? He steps up to the string and inspects it from a distance. He looks at where it connects to the ceiling. It doesn't seem to attach to anything, but could he be wrong after such a long time? He touches it very gently, but recoils his hand straight away. He is sure he felt something move. Or maybe it was just the string. He touches it again and it sways and comes to a stop. Nothing. He tugs it now very gently. Nothing. His anxiety is very high now, so he takes a short break, looking at the string again. It really doesn't seem to be connected to anything – like it is stuck to the ceiling with glue. OK, this is it. He pulls the string and it comes away in his hand. It sits there, static, in his palm. Nothing else happens. He waits, but nothing happens. He steps outside to a new day, to the start of a change in his life. His mansion is still there, and he still has it a year later.

This man had believed what he was told by the executor of the will and not questioned it, and changed his life hugely to fit around it. He had ended up convincing himself that something terrible would happen if he touched the piece of string. Eventually, he built up the confidence to inspect and understand the situation more closely, and to challenge his belief, and it was proved false. The moral of the story is this – it was these steps that he made to challenge his beliefs that were critical to his recovery. Later sections of the book aim to shed light on the beliefs you have that are making things difficult for you, and to encourage you to question them, and gradually to find other, less threatening, ways to view the world. Appendix 3 provides some more examples of analogies about anxiety like the one above.

Following are some other examples of vicious cycles to show how they can apply to different experiences. They are simple versions of models developed by cognitive therapists such as David M. Clark, Paul Salkovskis and Adrian Wells, who have used them to guide CBT for anxiety problems. In each example, it is the extreme thinking that seems to convert a normal reaction to stress into something more serious, and lead to behaviours that make the situation worse. Note that these examples will only apply to a small number of people – your own cycle will be different because it will contain your own particular situations, inner experiences, beliefs and behaviours.

A panic cycle

The first example shows how feelings of tightness in the chest that are actually caused by over-breathing can lead someone to breathe faster because they think that the tightness is actually a sign of suffocation. It is not – in this case it is muscle pain from over-breathing. This over-breathing then creates more of the pains, and so on. In addition, if the person avoids any exercise because of these fears, each time they encounter even a small amount of physical exertion, these feelings will return again, in a way they would not have done, had they exercised regularly.

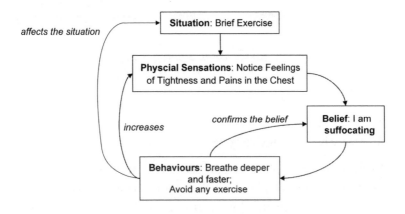

A social anxiety cycle

In this example, a person avoids looking at other people because they believe they will be ridiculed as a nervous wreck. Instead they focus on themselves and their bodily sensations to try to control them. There are several effects. First, the person believes that the reason they are not rejected by other people is because they have managed to hide their anxiety this time. But what about next time? Second, some of these safety behaviours make them feel more anxious – for example by focusing on their own bodies rather than looking at other people, these feelings seem much more noticeable. They have a 'felt sense' that other people can see their anxiety and are judging them because of it. Third, by avoiding eye contact and making efforts to hide their anxiety, they are making the situation more difficult for themselves – spending less time engaging with other people and focusing on the topic of the conversation.

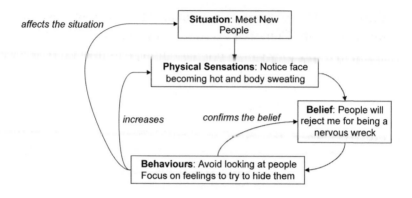

An obsessive-compulsive cycle

In the third example, a person gets an intrusive thought while holding a friend's baby – that they could throw the baby to the ground and harm it. This person strongly believes that this thought is unacceptable and a sign of being an evil person, so understandably tries to suppress it in any way possible – in this example by counting silently to twenty and avoiding this kind of situation in future. By doing this every time the thought arises, the person comes to believe that without counting, they might actually throw a baby to the ground. What's more, this counting behaviour does not work in the long term, and the thoughts come back another time. Avoiding these situations, leads to becoming more and more out of practice with them, to the point where any situation involving a baby or child triggers these thoughts. Again, the key to this cycle is the belief and the safety behaviour. If the person can gradually drop the safety behaviours and test the threatening belief, the cycle will start to be changed.

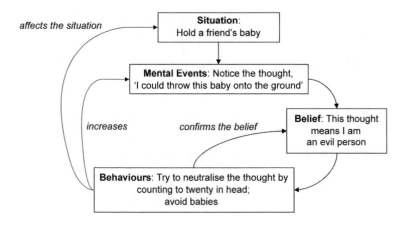

Stepping outside the cycle

In each of the above examples it is learning to accept and understand the physical sensation or mental event as a normal response that any of us could experience that is key. Appendix 1 provides normal explanations of many of these experiences. However, to accept these normal explanations we need to begin to let go of our habits, our usual ways of thinking about these experiences and reacting to them. A key part of the cycle is that we believe things because we have evidence for them from our own experience or from what we have been told. So, a major part of this book will be about how to identify what you believe and evaluate the evidence. For example, a person may have the thought: 'I will faint in the supermarket', for which the evidence is a feeling of weakness in their legs. They could consider other alternatives, such as, 'I will feel weak for a while and then recover' or, 'I am unlikely to faint', the evidence being that they have not fainted in the supermarket before, and they have felt weakness in their legs at home and not fainted. As mentioned before, learning to cope is not as simple as this example might suggest – this is just one technique of many!

In particular, we need time to pause and reflect to be able to question our beliefs. Where we focus our attention can be very important. By considering things that we don't normally focus on we get a wider view of the world, and more choice in our life. In chapter 7 I will introduce the ten-step plan, this will provide you with a different way of dealing with a feared situation than your previous ways of thinking and reacting to it, including focusing your attention in ways that help you to step outside a vicious cycle. Over time you can practise this more, starting with mild situations, and gradually working up to more challenging situations.

An example of how Janet faced her fear

> I booked a boat journey to Ireland which I found easier than a plane, but still my heart raced. The return journey had to be by plane because the boats had stopped sailing. At the airport I felt sheer panic, but I said to myself, 'The fear is not going to win.' I ran up the steps and got to my seat and I felt terrible as the engine started. But as the plane took off I got this strange feeling of excitement. The lady next to me said, 'Oh I hate this,' as the wheels moved under us, and I ended up telling her not to worry. After the plane landed, and as I walked through the airport with my case, I felt I had achieved the impossible and felt ten feet tall. Looking back at this experience, it was as though this feeling of confidence was my reward for being brave and facing my fear.

Below is a vicious cycle with blank boxes, for you to complete with your own experiences during a situation that makes you feel anxious. This may be easy to do now, or may make more sense later when you have read more of the book.

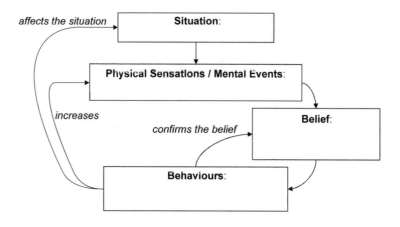

A 'virtuous' cycle?

When people start to step outside their vicious cycles, by thinking and behaving in different ways, they can start to develop a virtuous cycle of recovery. In practice, people will spend a fair bit of time going between vicious and virtuous cycles but each time a person goes into a virtuous cycle, they are building up their coping techniques. The diagrams on the next pages show how virtuous cycles can work, helping the person to learn to tolerate their experiences, think and behave in different ways, and gradually manage their distress better and increase their sense of confidence. In each case, the beliefs and behaviours are different from the vicious cycles, but the situations, physical sensations and mental events are the same. The new behaviours often involve just dropping the safety behaviours that formed the vicious cycle. They therefore involve facing some anxiety rather than trying to suppress it. This new approach gradually helps the person find evidence for alternative beliefs about the same physical sensations and mental events, leading the person to gradually face more challenging situations over time.

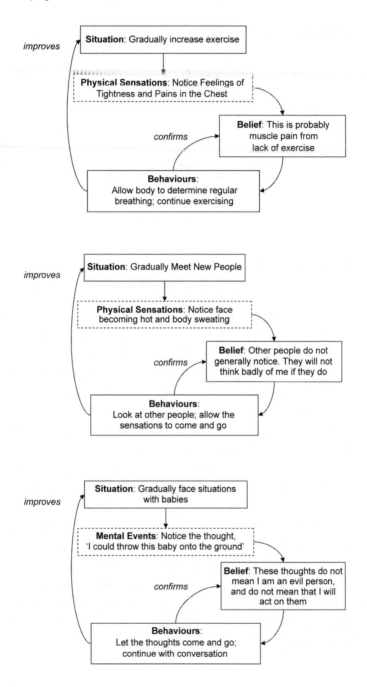

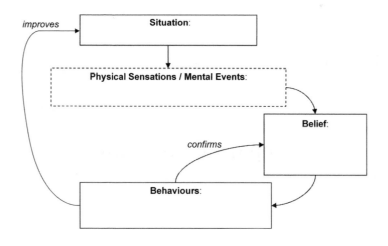

Key points

- Everyone occasionally experiences unusual thoughts, feelings and images that seem to come to them suddenly.
- Some people focus on these experiences and have worrying beliefs about them, whereas other people find it easier to ignore them. When people have extreme beliefs about their experiences, they tend to react in unhelpful ways that can make the situation worse.
- The vicious cycle of mental events, threat beliefs and behaviour, may explain why some people's problems with anxiety continue.
- By considering things that we don't normally focus on we can get a wider view of the world and start to question certain ideas we may have.
- People can learn to step outside vicious cycles by focusing on different things in their surroundings, thinking of other possible reasons for their experiences, and by trying out new ways of coping.
- A virtuous cycle is a way of plotting what is helping you to cope better.

6

Preparing for change

The willingness to accept responsibility for one's own life is the source from which self-respect springs.

Joan Didion

Before introducing the programme aimed at preparing you for change, I need to say something about change, and how to know when you are ready. It is possible that you have already started to consider the ideas in this book, and to think about change. It is also possible that the idea of change still seems like a distant possibility. The rate at which different people learn to cope with their fears varies widely. And everyone finds change difficult to some degree. There are many times when people return to their earlier habits of thinking and behaving. For one thing, the experiences that make us anxious are very persuasive; they tend to make us react immediately, in habitual ways; these are instant attempts to reach safety. The aim of this book is to provide a space to slow down and try something different.

Fear of change

Change can feel very frightening in itself. Keeping things as they are feels safe, and to a certain degree this is true. 'Sticking with what you know' is a good rule of thumb. You may have decided that even a small change is too much for you at the moment. It is worth thinking about what very small change you might be willing to accept. Change is part of life. Our bodies change over time. Other people change over time. New people come into our life and familiar people sometimes leave us. We all deal with small changes, and we may often do it without really noticing. Change can often involve learning and becoming stronger. How small a change are you willing to accept? To think that some of your distressing experiences might be normal? To stay with your feelings of anxiety for just a second longer before trying to control them?

The idea of change can sound frightening to some people. However, it may be worth weighing up the changes you might make from learning to cope better against the changes you may have already made. Many people with anxiety problems have already changed all kinds of things to accommodate their fears – where they travel, who they see, where they shop, the jobs they have, and many other aspects of their lives. Actually then, change may not be so new. And taking an active choice to make a change that you want to make, despite your anxiety, can seem less ominous when you think of these earlier changes you may already have made. This time, if you are willing, it could be an opportunity to gradually reclaim some of your life.

No one can force you to change. And if other people try, they often get it wrong because they don't know you as well as you know yourself. You know your thoughts, your feelings and your memories. Therefore, you are in the best position to make a change, when, and only when, you are ready. What I can try to do in this guide is provide you with information that you can use, and put into practice, to help you get better when you choose to.

Some people think that men and women with fears and phobias are not motivated enough to overcome their fears. This is a very simplistic way of seeing the human mind. What seems more true to people's experience is very different. People with fears and phobias can be extremely motivated to overcome their fears and be terrified of facing them at the same time. In fact, sometimes it seems that being extremely motivated, or being pushed to do things, can increase the anxiety further. How does this happen?

Throughout the book, we have seen that anxiety is caused by people's explanation of their experiences, and nothing to do with not trying hard enough. Actually, people often go to extreme lengths to try to avoid what they fear – they must be motivated to do this. However, we have seen how trying too hard can make things worse, leading people to criticise themselves for not eliminating their distress or doing as well as they had planned. The approach of this book is based on the idea that people are already in conflict between what they want to do and what they fear might happen. The simple model of not being sufficiently motivated does not apply. So, changing may not require you to try hard at all, but just to consider different ways of seeing and doing things.

One way to start to think about whether you are ready to change is to consider the advantages and disadvantages of coping with your fears. You could use the table below to note down your ideas. It is important to think of the things that will be good for you, not what you think other people believe you should do. What is it that you would like to do if you were to learn to cope better with your anxiety? You may want to go into some situations that you find difficult at the moment (for example, shops, public transport, parties), meet people you haven't seen for a while, or develop new skills and hobbies.

Then have a think about what is holding you back from starting to cope with your fears. What do you think might have to happen for you to learn to cope with your anxiety better? Could you miss out on time spent doing other things? Might you have to stop doing something that seems to have helped you for years? What do you think might happen if you become more able to cope? Might you lose out on something that you have already? Does changing mean something specific to you? Something that you are afraid of or worried about?

It is clearly difficult for me as the author of this book to imagine what might be the very personal concerns you have about change. However, it is my experience that most people do have them, as well as reasons for wanting to change. People have conflicting beliefs. It is the normal way to be. I like chocolate but too much of it gives me spots. I want to go on holiday but I am worried about missing work that I need to do. We all have conflicts and just trying harder is not the way to solve them. Solving them comes from first accepting the conflict, then understanding it properly, and only after this can a possible solution come to mind. Even then, that's not the end of it because new conflicts will arise in the future. People lead complex lives and this richness of experience is part of being human.

Table 6.1 The pros and cons of change

What might I gain from learning to cope with my anxiety better?	What might be the disadvantages of learning to cope with my anxiety better?
1.	1.
2.	2.
3.	3.
4.	4.
5.	5.

Conflicting beliefs about change – Paul

When I started therapy, I felt a big pressure to change. I was doing all these things to keep safe – avoiding groups of lads, going out only when it was quiet, wearing a big jacket and not getting caught staring at people. They were keeping me safe (I thought), but they were also making my life hell. My therapist talked about 'dropping my safety behaviours', but this was a big jump for me. I had been like this for years. Sometimes just talking about it all seemed too much. It was when I went on a trip with my therapist to the shops that I started to change. We took the risk of looking people in the eyes and going into busy places. One time, a burly man came up to us and I was convinced 'this was it' – the attack I was waiting for – but he asked us for directions! There were times when the anxiety just seemed too much to bear on these trips and I wanted to give up. However, I learnt over time to face these feelings and find out that my neighbourhood was not as dangerous as I had thought. I can get round the shops now when I want. I would still like to move though – it's not like it's completely safe.

Each small step is progress

At some time you are likely to come to the point that you decide to try to make a change. You could try to make a large change or a small change. It is up to you. However, the larger the change you make, the more likely it is that you will make a mistake or suffer a setback. On the other hand, if you make a very tiny change, you might feel unsatisfied. It seems as though either way, there is a risk of being hard on yourself. So, you need to be prepared. If you take things gradually, you need to be prepared to notice and acknowledge the small progress you make, praising yourself in the process. If you make bigger changes, you need to be prepared for not getting things quite right and experiencing a setback. Understandably, this can be upsetting, but try not to make more of it than it is. Each time you lapse, you have the memory of what happened, and you can use this to try to do things differently next time. There might even be a section in the book that is relevant to the setback. The important message here is, whatever pace of change you take, you are more likely to progress in the long run if you are kind to yourself and acknowledge what you have managed.

Personal example of taking small steps – Paul

I faced my memories of the assault a little bit at time. First, I gradually talked about what had happened to my therapist, who listened carefully and I really valued this. Next, I talked to my friend about it. I was surprised how well he listened too, and he didn't dismiss my fears. There were still some things that happened before the assault that were too upsetting to think about, so I didn't talk about them until I could trust people better. The next step though was to go back to where I was assaulted. This was a big step for me, and I think I only managed it because I had begun to deal with the memories first and talk about them. Going back to the scene helped because I could try to piece together what had happened. I had been convinced that I was to blame for what had happened because of what I had said under my breath to the drunken lad just before he went for me. When I went back though, I realised that he could not have heard me from that distance – so it wasn't my fault. That helped a lot. I have some more steps I want to take such as going to the pub. The plan is to start at a quiet time during the day, then some time in the future I may get to go to my local pub in the evening when it's busy and meet my friend there for a drink.

Key points

- It is normal to be afraid of change.
- People with fears and phobias can be extremely motivated to

overcome their fears and be terrified of facing their fears at the same time.

- Change can often involve learning and becoming stronger.
- Each small step is progress.
- You are in the best position to know when to make a change.

7

Developing your own programme for coping

All life is an experiment. The more experiments you make the better.

Ralph Waldo Emerson

You gain strength, courage, and confidence by every experience in which you really stop to look fear in the face. Try to do the thing which you think you cannot do.

Eleanor Roosevelt

You don't have to see the whole staircase, just take the first step.

Martin Luther King Jr

This chapter provides a ten-step plan to coping with fears and phobias. It relies on putting together all that you have read in the previous chapters, so you may want to refresh yourself with these again. I will go through each stage in the text and then a table is provided for you to photocopy or download to use as a template for each situation that you face. Try to work through the sheet a step at a time. The ten-step plan is designed for each stage of progress that you make – each of these stages is a step towards coping better with your fears. Appendix 3 provides a table for you to record each goal that you make a ten-step plan for, and record what you learn from attempting it.

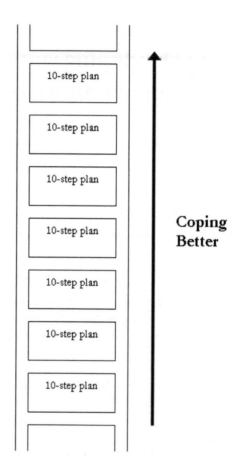

The ten-step plan

Why could the ten-step plan work for you? A plan that takes a few pages to explain may seem too simple to deal with a set of complex problems. What reasons are there to think that it would work? The first reason is that simple, systematic methods are nearly always what are used to solve intricate problems in the outside world, like unravelling a knot of wool a loop at a time, or navigating using a compass. So, maybe they work for complex psychological problems too. The second reason is that the plan is designed to help you put into practice what you have read in the earlier chapters – so it is not just the plan that helps by itself, but the fact that it leads you to draw on and try out what you have read. The third reason is that the plan is designed to follow, as closely as possible, the way that effective psychologists work with people to help them cope with their anxiety during therapy – and these methods have been shown to work. The fourth and final reason is that the plan fits well with much broader theories about human behaviour that, if you are interested, you can read about in some of the other books included in the reading list in appendix 5. Of course, there are no guarantees that it will work for you, but what have you got to lose by giving it a try?

1. Choosing a situation to face

Your first step towards starting to cope may need to be a small one. Whenever we believe that there is a new danger, our body secretes some adrenaline. However, if we focus on the same thing for a while, and there are no further threats, no more adrenaline is secreted. Your body will naturally break this adrenaline down over several minutes. So, the feelings of anxiety will gradually subside. The body needs time to do this. And it needs the person to face a mild fear that they can focus on, rather than something so frightening that they will start worrying more and try to escape. This is one reason why the programme is split into small, achievable steps.

It is a good idea to make the first step you choose one that you have tried to face before, and one that is much less threatening than some recent frightening situations that you have found yourself in. This time you are going to choose to face the situation. Below are some examples of situations that people choose early on in learning to cope. Some of these may be right for you:

- Trying to face a situation that can sometimes make you anxious but that you have tried before. This might mean going into a situation with people around, or stepping outside your 'safe zone' for a short while.
- Noticing a sensation in your body (for example, a pain) that you may normally try to avoid, or that you normally think about but do not normally focus on and really feel for any length of time.
- Looking at a drawing of something you are afraid of.
- Looking at a photograph of something you are afraid of. Some photographs are more anxiety-provoking than others. Start with one that is not very frightening for you.

When you plan the situation you are going to face, try to be as specific as possible, so that you know exactly what your goal is. In particular, be clear where you will be, when you are planning to do this, and, importantly, how long you will do it for. It can be very useful to plan how much time you will spend in the situation. This helps to ensure that you leave the situation when you have decided to, rather than because of how you feel at the time. Even if you feel that you could stay longer in a situation, stick to your decision and finish when you had planned. In this way you will have achieved your first step. You can take a break, be pleased with yourself, and save your next step for another time. The temptation to stay longer in a situation than you had planned may be an example of you pushing yourself more, thinking 'this is not good enough' or, 'I must try harder.' There is no need. If you reach your target then this is enough. Your next step can wait for another day. In this way you can begin to make choices that are not based on your feelings in that moment, but on what you have decided. Another good thing about giving yourself an exact time in a situation is that you can start with brief periods (like staying in a public place where you feel anxious for only one minute). The next time, when you are ready, you could try two minutes.

Remember that the first situation you face can seem very small. It just needs to be something that you feel able to deal with. For example, some people may find a photograph of what they are afraid of too disturbing, so a drawing, cartoon, or even just the word itself can be a good start.

It is helpful to measure your anxiety during the situation. This will help you see how your anxiety changes over periods of seconds or minutes, as well as seeing how your anxiety to the same situation changes over periods of days, weeks and months. The table includes a rating scale from 0 to 10, in which 0 would be 'not at all anxious' and 10 would correspond to 'extreme panic'. Most people find it useful to aim for a manageable level of anxiety that is still a challenge. So, as a useful rule of thumb, try for a situation that you would rate between 2 and 7. Remember, the aim of the exposure is not to reduce your feelings of anxiety, although this may happen. The aim is to stay in a situation despite your anxiety. Within the range of 2–7, there is likely to be enough anxiety to be a challenge, but not so much that it would feel overwhelming.

2. Physical sensations and mental events

It is very important to note, as mentioned in earlier chapters, that very often it is not the frightening thing in the outside world that people are afraid of. It is the experiences that this thing triggers in their mind and body. Sometimes these events can come on suddenly and grab a person's attention. So, it is better to be prepared for this in advance, and to include these physical sensations and mental events in your programme. If you expect the situation that you plan to face to trigger physical sensations and mental events, write these down too. For a start, it makes it clear just how much you are taking on in your first step – not just the situation itself but the experiences it triggers inside you. This makes it all the more important to start with a small step that is familiar to you. However, this time you are going to face it differently, because you will be expecting these physical feelings and mental events too. Some examples include:

- A physical sensation, ache or pain in your body.
- Thoughts that pop into your mind that you normally try to suppress.
- Memories that pop into your mind that you normally try to get rid of.
- Visual images or pictures that come into your mind.
- Impulses to say or do things that seem unacceptable to you.
- Things that you can hear but other people cannot.

These are all thoughts or feelings that come to you suddenly, out of your own control, rather than things you might do in your head more deliberately, like choosing to distract yourself. If any of these experiences usually occur when you go into a feared situation, write them down, and describe them in enough detail so that when you read them later, they are familiar to you. Remember that the idea is that you are going to choose to face these physical sensations and mental events rather than feeling drawn in by them or having to avoid them. So, if you think that this may be too big a step for now, go back again and think of a different situation – one that triggers physical sensations and mental events that are more manageable. It doesn't matter how minor or harmless the situation might seem to other people. Only you know what inner experiences it leads to, so only you are in a position to know what the first manageable step might be.

3. Writing down your 'extreme threat' beliefs

This next step helps you to express what you are really frightened about. It involves writing down what you believe might happen if you were to face the situation, along with the physical sensations and mental events that it triggers. You are trying to identify your 'worst fear'. People vary a great deal in how able they are to express what they are afraid of happening. One difference seems to be how willing they are to admit that they have this fear – because it seems irrational or odd when they tell other people, or even say it to themselves. One good thing about using a self-help guide is that you don't have to tell anyone except yourself. Here are some prompts that may help you get to your worst fear:

- What do you think is the worst thing that could happen if you faced the situation? Or if you couldn't escape?
- What is the worst thing that could happen if you faced the distressing physical sensations and mental events that you get in the situation?
- Try to imagine starting to step into this situation. What are you starting to worry might happen to you?
- Do you have a picture in your head of what might happen to you?
- Do you fear that you might go through something extremely distressing that you have been through before, or that someone close to you has been through?
- What would this look like?
- How would you know if it were to happen?

The idea is to be able to express a prediction that is genuinely an extreme threat. I would expect your belief to actually match how frightened you get in the situation. If anyone else believed what you do in this situation, would they be just as anxious as you? If the answer is 'yes' then you have probably found your worst fear. If the answer is 'no' then you may not have expressed it quite right. For example if I were to take a flight on a jet aircraft, I may fear that I won't be able to cope with the anxiety. But what does 'not coping' really mean to me? Actually, when I really imagine going on that plane, I have an image of myself losing control of my behaviour and being restrained by the other passengers, and then being rejected and shunned by them. This is my worst case scenario which I 'fast-forward' to, and I have a vivid image of it in my mind – and this is what I am really thinking might happen. I can now begin to understand why I get anxious on planes. Of course the worst case scenario is very different for different people. Your worst fear will be different, depending on your past experiences and what is going on for you at the moment.

The questions should help you to identify what you think is the worst thing that could happen. The next stage is to rate how much you believe this. It may be that you think this is very unlikely to happen in the first step you have suggested. However, if you even believe it a tiny amount then this is a start – you can test this belief out for the first time rather than behaving as if it actually might be true. The table includes a section to note the 'percentage belief rating'. So, if you are convinced, that would be 100 per cent, and 50 per cent would be that there is a 50:50 chance of it happening – the same as the chance of a coin coming up 'heads'. A score of 0 per cent is reserved for when you are convinced that the worst fear would never happen.

4. Alternative, less threatening beliefs

Here is the chance to write down what you would like to believe, and how you would like the situation to turn out. What would someone who is not afraid believe might happen in this situation? These alternative beliefs don't have to be really positive. They just need to reflect a bad thing not happening, and possibly a good thing in its place. Some examples might be:

- I can face my feelings.
- The situation is not harmful or dangerous.
- I managed to get through the situation.

- I managed to achieve something I have wanted to do for a while.
- Other people respond well to me.

You could think of other examples using the explanations in appendix 1 and the self-soothing statements in chapter 3.

5. Preparing to face the situation

Preparing for the situation is really just to make sure that you can approach it in the way that you have planned. Planning is important, because it helps to put you in control of what you will do when you face the situation. One way to help this happen is to plan when you are going to face the situation, and give yourself a few minutes beforehand to read through what you have written down under points 1–4 in your coping plan. At the back of this book, appendix 3 provides some analogies that may help you imagine how you will face the situation. It also helps you to expect to do what you have written down and be ready for it. Things may not go exactly as you had planned, but there is space to deal with that later. Now you are prepared, it is time to make the first small step.

6. Facing the situation

Now you are putting your plan into practice. Here are a few things to look out for:

- *Last minute avoidance.* You may want to avoid doing this right at the last minute – could you have set your first step too high? Remember it is entirely your choice where you place that first step. Is it your feelings of anxiety that are making you want to turn back? If so, face them now, focus on the feeling in your body. Keep your attention there. What are your feelings now? Do you want them to determine what you do, or do you want to stick to what you have planned?

- *Changing goals.* It can be tempting to change your goals when you are in the situation. If you planned, for example, to look at a picture of a spider for five seconds, and that's what you managed, stop there. Praise yourself. Relax and take a break. Don't try to look at the picture for any longer than you had planned. There is no rush. If however, you find your goal too difficult to achieve it is OK to change it for another time. For example, you may find an alternative goal that is more manageable at the moment.

- *Drifting attention.* Is your attention drifting to thoughts in your head rather than focusing on the moment? As I have mentioned in earlier chapters, a key part of facing your fears is really facing them, and that means focusing your attention on what you are afraid of, and what it feels like, looks like or sounds like. Try to focus on the moment. If you are confronting a dog, are you really focusing on the dog, looking at it, seeing its eyes, its nose, its fur and its teeth? Maybe you find certain parts of the dog more threatening. That's OK. You will probably just need more time to learn to cope with them. If you are focusing on your feelings of anxiety, are you really focusing on your feelings of anxiety, on that buzzing feeling, maybe on the feeling of tension in your stomach, or in your limbs? If you are then that is great. You are learning to cope. If not, and your mind is somewhere else, or on your thoughts, then you are probably not really focusing on the physical sensations of anxiety. That's OK, just focus back on those sensations in your body again and see what happens.

- *Trying to control the feelings.* It can be tempting to try to suppress the physical feelings of anxiety. However, the plan is to try to face them. For example, anxiety can be seen as a wave. Imagine you are in a boat on a shallow lake. If a wave approaches, you can't stop it or control it. You have to accept that it is coming. And when it comes towards you, you can ride it out, float with it and allow it to pass you.

- *Peaks of anxiety and other mental events.* Sometimes the anxiety might reach a peak that you hadn't expected. It can help, when anxiety seems overwhelming, to take your mind away from your worrying thoughts and onto your surroundings. Take in what is around you. This can help you to 'ground' yourself again. Some people find it useful to ground themselves on an object like a squeezable sponge ball. Remember though, this is a coping strategy to deal with an unexpected peak of anxiety that you would not need to use for more mild anxiety. It does not get rid of anxiety, but allows you to focus your attention back again on the outside world. You might also choose to use this technique if you get a particularly sudden ache or pain that captures and holds your attention. You can ground yourself on an object in the outside world for a while and then bring your attention back to the feeling when you are ready. You may find that choosing to focus on these feelings at your own pace is a very different experience from having your attention captured by them at first. By choosing what to focus on, you are beginning to take control of the anxiety, rather than it controlling you. Of course, I would not expect you to feel that you always had to squeeze a sponge ball to keep safe – it is something that you might try to help cope with overwhelming physical feelings on occasion, and then reduce the use of it over time. For more details about focusing your attention, you may want to have a look at the section on BMR again (chapter 3).

Good luck with putting your programme into practice! Remember, if it doesn't go according to plan, you can deal with this in the next stage.

7. Unpredicted experiences

It is rare that facing your fears in this way goes exactly as planned, whatever your level of preparation. Maybe the situation wasn't quite how you expected. Or you may have experienced physical sensations or mental events that you did not expect. You may also have found yourself doing things that you hadn't planned. If you write these unexpected things down, it gives you the chance to try to understand these kinds of situations for the future. It can also help you to choose the most appropriate situations for next time. Sometimes the unexpected events can be positive ones – for example, you might have found that other people responded better than you had thought they might, or that you found yourself doing something that seemed helpful. However, at other times the unexpected events can seem like a setback.

If the situation did turn out worse than you had expected, it is worth asking yourself, did I do something to change the situation and make it different? This can sometimes happen. For example, if you were hyperventilating, this may have given you unusual sensations. Also, you may have been doing something that you thought might have been keeping you safe, but could have changed the situation. One example is a person with a phobia of spiders who set the goal of touching a jar that had a motionless spider inside it. She tried to touch the jar very quickly which jerked the jar and made the spider move suddenly. Now she was facing a moving spider rather than a motionless one – a more challenging situation. There are other examples of this type of problem in the previous chapter where vicious cycles are introduced. It is very understandable to respond in these ways. The important thing is to note these differences and to acknowledge that the situation was different from what you had expected. You may be able to learn from this.

8. What happened?

In this section of the table, you write down what actually happened. The aim is to write down exactly what went on, rather than what you thought about it. What did you do? What did you see or hear? What happened to the anxiety? If you were writing this situation as a scene in a movie, how would you tell the actors where to stand, and what to do and say? Detail is the key.

9. Revisiting your predictions

Now you can return to your predictions and beliefs. Did your worst case scenario happen? Did anything happen to suggest that your extreme threat belief might be true? Did anything happen to suggest that your alternative beliefs might be true? Go back to sections 3 and 4 and rate each of them again in the table. At this point you can write down what you feel you have learnt from the experience. You may have learnt that your worst fear did not come true. You may have learnt that you sometimes do things that can make the situation worse.

10. Being kind to yourself

The step you take could turn out in different ways. It might seem like a complete success, a complete failure, or somewhere in between. Whatever happened, you made a start, and you have begun to learn how to face your fears. You could do something to give yourself a break for now, then, another day, you can return to section 1 and think about the next step. For now, just do something else you want to do. It can be helpful to identify what you have learnt, and what strengths you have drawn on to make this step. Chapter 11 provides ways that you can identify and record these strengths, values and resources. It can also be helpful to start to plot your virtuous cycles (see the last chapter) – the ways of thinking and behaving you have tried that have started to work.

Returning to step 1

Depending on what happened you will have an idea of what the next step might be. It could be the same situation again, but taking account of what you have learnt. This is fine. If the situation still makes you anxious then you can stick with this one and continue learning how to cope using these steps. Alternatively, you may want to make the same situation slightly more challenging, by slightly increasing how anxious it would make you feel. For example, you could stay longer, or you could focus on your feelings a bit more rather than trying to control them.

Using the ten-step plan for other goals

The plan lends itself to some other ways of learning to cope. An alternative way to use the ten-step plan is for other goals that you have that may not actually make you anxious, but that you have been avoiding doing. For example, if you are experiencing physical problems such as chronic pain or chronic fatigue, it may seem impossible to do anything because of your physical difficulties. The ten-step plan allows you to set one small goal at a time, to see how it goes, and to gradually build up your activity a small amount at a time. For example, reading a book can be split up into reading a page at a time, or the task of cleaning the house can be divided into cleaning one room, or only one piece of furniture in a room at a time. This may seem laborious, but it often leads to more progress than setting the complete goal ('I must tidy the whole house today!') which seems daunting and so may not even be started. This way you can get started. Other plans that can be tackled using this scheme include cutting down smoking, and revising for exams. You may, however, need to tackle any self-critical thoughts you have about your pace of progress (see the next chapter). The key is to acknowledge and praise yourself for each step completed, and take a step back and re-evaluate your goals if you have a setback.

Another way to use the ten-step plan comes after you have already tried it several times and are making some progress. At this stage, you might try to face a more difficult situation and make a stronger test of your 'extreme threat' beliefs. One technique that can be very helpful for people at this stage is to actively 'bring on' the anxiety. So, instead of trying to limit how anxious you feel, you do things to bring on the anxiety itself. For example, a person who is afraid of suffocating could actively try to hold their breath when inside a supermarket. A person who is afraid of being contaminated would actively bring on their anxiety by touching a toilet bowl. When doing so, be sure to write down what the worst thing that could happen would be. At this stage, if a person can tolerate the anxiety that they have brought on themselves and still cope well with the situation, it further increases their confidence and sense of control. They start to realize that they can cope with more anxiety than they had thought, they realize that the 'worst' thing doesn't usually happen, and they often identify more of their own skills and resources than they had expected. These kinds of situations can be monitored using the same ten-step plan. Of course, this stage comes with time, and it is by no means appropriate for everyone. Yet, for some people, it can have some of the biggest effects on learning to cope and overcoming the problems caused by anxiety.

Table 7.1 Ten-step plan record sheet

---

1. The situation

Think of a situation that would make you feel anxious.
    If possible, imagine it in your mind's eye.
How anxious would this make you feel? 0 = not at all and
    10 = extreme panic.
If the answer is 8 or more then think of a smaller step, or a less
    anxiety-provoking situation. It can be as simple as looking
    at a certain object or picture for a set amount of time.
Situation . . . .
How long do I plan to stay in the situation? . . . .

How anxious do I think it will make me feel? 0 1 2 3 4 5 6 7 8 9 10

Are you sure that this goal is manageable? If not try going back again and making the goal simpler. Remember, you want to try to take this step as it has been described here, no more and no less.

2. Physical sensations and mental events that are expected

What kinds of physical sensations might you expect? What kinds of mental events would you expect to pop into your head during this situation?

Examples include: images, memories, feelings, sounds, impulses and thoughts. List them and describe how you might experience them:

. . . .

. . . .

. . . .

. . . .

. . . .

3. Your 'extreme threat' beliefs

What is the worst thing that you think might happen if you go into this situation and experience the physical sensations and mental events listed above? What do you fear would actually happen? Try to imagine this scenario. How much do you believe each of these ideas from 0% (not at all) to 100% (completely sure)? Only put down up to 3 of your most extreme beliefs here, not ones that you think might be reasonable for anyone to have in this situation.

Extreme threat belief 1:

. . . .

. . . .

. . . . % Before . . . . After . . . .

Extreme threat belief 2:

. . . .

. . . .

. . . . % Before . . . . After . . . .

Extreme threat belief 3:

. . . .

. . . .

. . . . % Before . . . . After . . . .

4. Alternative beliefs

What would the best outcome of this situation be? Might there be a less threatening outcome? What might someone else who is not afraid of this situation believe about it? Is there a less threatening way of thinking about these physical sensations and mental events? Do you believe that they are a normal response to stress that might not be harmful in any way? Write down up to 3 of these beliefs. How much do you believe each of these less threatening ideas?

Alternative belief 1:

....

....

.... % Before .... After ....

Alternative belief 2:

....

....

.... % Before .... After ....

Alternative belief 3:

....

....

.... % Before .... After ....

5. Preparing to face the situation

Read points 1 to 4 above. Are there any changes you need to make?
Are you ready to focus your attention on the situation and notice the bodily sensations and mental events you are expecting? Are you ready and willing to stay with these without trying to control them?
Remind yourself of how long you are planning to face this situation for. Remember the idea is to experience the things you have described rather than to distract yourself from them or try to control them in some way. Are you ready to do this? If not, you can consider changing the goal to a smaller step.

6. Facing the situation

Did I face that situation as planned? Yes / No.
If you ticked 'Yes' then well done. Go to 8 and then continue.
If you ticked 'No' then well done. Go to 7 and then continue.

7. Unpredicted experiences

A common reason for not facing the situation is that something happened that you had not predicted, or you did something that you hadn't planned on doing. Is this the case? It may be that you didn't focus your attention on the situation but you started to go through other thoughts in your mind. If any of these occurred, in what ways was the situation different from what you had expected?

. . . .
. . . .
. . . .
. . . .
. . . .
. . . .

8. What happened?

What happened as the situation unfolded? After you spent the time in the situation that you had planned, what happened at the end? You can put 'nothing', or something good or bad that happened. Be sure to put down what actually happened, what you saw, heard or felt, rather than what you thought about it.

. . . .
. . . .
. . . .
. . . .
. . . .

9. Revisiting your predictions

Look again at sections 3 and 4, bearing in mind what happened in the situation. Now rate each of the beliefs again. Was there any change? If so, what does this mean about how certain you can be of these ideas? If not, what do you think might help you change these beliefs in the future? How could you start to set up a situation like this, or that goes a small way towards it?

In your own words, what did you learn from trying to face this situation:

. . . .
. . . .

. . . .
. . . .
. . . .

10. Being kind to yourself and taking a break

Whatever the outcome, you have a right to be somewhat pleased with
yourself. You can take a break now, get on with other things, and
return to the next situation you want to try out at another time.
You could record the strengths and resources you have used. Well
done!

If things haven't gone as planned, you may feel inclined to criticise or
blame yourself or someone else. This would be understandable, but
bear in mind that it will have a negative effect on your mood if you
dwell on it for long. Although it is often difficult, you are the person with the ultimate responsibility for the mood you are in. Think
about whether you are ready to change right now (chapter 6), and
then come back to this chapter when you feel ready. Chapters 8–10
deal with other commonly encountered obstacles – see if they can
help. Above all, praise yourself for continuing to work at it.

Table 7.2 Ten-step plan progress sheet

	What situation did I face?	What did I learn?
Ten-step plan 1 Date		
Ten-step plan 2 Date		
Ten-step plan 3 Date		
Ten-step plan 4 Date		
Ten-step plan 5 Date		

Ten-step plan 6
Date

Ten-step plan 7
Date

Ten-step plan 8
Date

Ten-step plan 9
Date

Ten-step plan 10
Date

Please note that the tables in this chapter are available to download from the companion website.

Key points

- A system like the ten-step plan can help you put what you have read into practice.
- The goals you choose can be as small as you like, and can include what you try to manage already.
- The plan allows you to record what you have managed, any difficulties, and what you can learn for the future.
- Later sections of the book will try to help you with other difficulties you encounter when trying to put your plan into practice.

8

Dealing with worry and self-blame

Worry gives a small thing a big shadow.

Swedish proverb

As a rule, what is out of sight disturbs men's minds more seriously than what they see.

Julius Caesar

For peace of mind, resign as general manager of the universe.

Author unknown

In previous chapters I have pointed to the problems of worrying, self-critical thinking, and spending time dwelling on negative aspects of ourselves. These can all be called 'rumination' or 'recurrent thinking'. Actually, just as fear is normal, so most people worry to some degree. However, this recurrent thinking can really get in the way of doing your ten-step programme because the thoughts take your attention away from what is really going on, from really noticing whether there are things to be afraid of or not. As this book is focused mainly on dealing with fears and phobias, it does not focus directly on these styles of thinking, but tries to explain how they make recovery from a phobia difficult. However, for some people these kinds of thinking seem to be their main problem. So, I have provided a brief chapter for dealing with them directly. Some readers may also be interested in checking out books that address recurrent thinking directly (see the reading list in appendix 5 – *The Worry Cure* by Bob Leahy is one example).

An example of worrying – Janet

> When my fears were at their worst, I worried that anything that could go wrong, would go wrong. If I had a headache, I thought it was a brain haemorrhage. If I had a stomach ache I thought it was my appendix. If my breathing got faster I thought I was going to die from a heart attack. When I was driving, I became convinced that the brakes might fail, a tyre might burst, or that I would suddenly go blind, cause an accident and leave my family without me. I still get these thoughts occasionally, but after facing my fear of travelling over several years, I now worry less about other things too.

What are worry and self-blame?

All these types of thinking can be called, 'recurrent negative thinking'. They are not occasional negative thoughts, which are very common. They are long chains of negative thoughts, typically about oneself or people close to oneself. These thoughts are typically in words, rather like talking to yourself in your own head – an 'inner dialogue'. Again, having an 'inner dialogue' is normal. It is how negative and extreme this dialogue tends to be that is the problem. People end up at places in their heads that they could never get to in reality – far into the future or back into the depths of the past. Whether any of this thinking is useful for the present, the here and now, is an open question. There certainly are drawbacks however. Here are some examples of the kinds of recurrent negative thinking that can go on in people's heads:

1. *Worry.* Worry is typically about predicting the worst things that could happen – it is the 'What if ...?' question played over and over again in a person's mind:

    'What if there is heavy traffic?'
    'I will be late for work.'
    'What if I am late for work?'
    'My boss will be angry with me.'
    'What if my boss is angry?'
    'I will lose my job.'

    Asking the 'What if ...?' question over and over like this leads a person to imagine more and more awful scenarios and become more anxious. Worry can therefore make a person anxious about a situation before they have even encountered it, and even if it never happens. Worry can take a person's thoughts so far into the future that they can imagine their own death even though they have all the rest of their life to lead right now. Although some worrying is normal, people who worry a great deal tend to be distressed with their worry and feel they have no control over it.

2. *Self-critical thinking.* This is the tendency to react to yourself with an 'attack' inside your own head. People attack themselves in different ways. For example, some people may insult themselves in their own minds: 'Idiot!' 'Pathetic!' 'Loser!' Sometimes people shout these words out to themselves. Other forms of self-criticism are more subtle: 'You have to try harder!' 'Get going or you'll lose it!' And yet others are more extreme: restricting or harming oneself in some way as a punishment. Very often people have picked up these ways of dealing with themselves from close people around them, and they feel that they help to keep them motivated and out of danger.

3. *Rumination.* Rumination involves thinking about how you feel at the moment and asking particular kinds of questions about it. One of these is the 'Why?' question:

'Why have I not done anything today?'
'Because I am lazy.'
'Why am I lazy?'
'Because I am a useless person.'

It seems that the 'Why?' question doesn't really lead to answers about negative moods – it only makes a person generate damaging, negative ideas about themselves from quite minor experiences. Rumination also includes thinking about trying to reinvent the past or replay the past. It is the 'If only ...' type of thinking: 'If only I had not taken the bus to work everything would have been OK.' This is a very common reaction to a traumatic event that could have been avoided. None of us can time-travel into the past and reverse it, yet this fact does not stop our minds from trying to do so.

Are worry and blaming yourself useful?

It seems to be the case that most people who worry, ruminate and self-criticise believe that doing it is helpful in some way. Some people may say that it helps them to solve their problems, to be reminded of their responsibilities, to be prepared for the worst, or to prevent disappointment. Often people say that they worry about one thing to distract themselves from more serious worries that they can't face. Often, when people are asked why they are hard on themselves, they say that they want to try to keep themselves safe and out of trouble. Do you believe some of these things? If so, that makes sense of why you might be thinking like this even though it leads to problems. It raises the question – is there another way that you could do things such as motivate yourself, without worrying or being hard on yourself? For example, could you use some of the strategies in this book instead?

It is often not possible to find out whether a thought we have is true or false. For example, if I am worried that I may lose my job in a year's time, there is no way to test this out right now. So, for many of our problematic styles of thinking, it is better to take a different tack. Is it helpful for me to think that I may lose my job in a year's time? Will it help me to work better or enjoy my life more? Maybe it would help me to be prepared for the worst? Or will it make me so anxious that it affects my job performance, so making it more likely I will lose it? People seem to do things like worrying because they believe that it helps them, but worry leads to problems in itself. So, could we give up worrying and replace it with another way of thinking about the future? If we can't predict the future, then why not imagine the positive things that might happen as much as the negative things? The more we imagine different things that might happen in the future the more we realise that we can't be particularly sure about any of them – there are so many possibilities: good, bad and in between. Very often recovery is about accepting this uncertainty about the future. Uncertainty is a fact of life but it takes time for us to learn to accept it.

Are worrying, self-criticism and rumination dangerous?

People whose main problem is this kind of thinking often believe that their worrying will be harmful in some way. They may think they will 'lose control of their mind', end up a 'nervous wreck' or that it will have serious physical effects. The cognitive therapist Adrian Wells has used the terms 'worry about worry' or 'meta-worry' for this kind of thinking. It seems as though worry about worry can make people even more anxious, yet it doesn't stop the worrying. Do you have worry about worry? How would you know if worry really caused all of these bad things? By trying to control the worry – worrying one day and not the next and seeing what happens? To do this, however, you would need to be able to control your worry.

People often believe that their worrying is uncontrollable, that once they have started they cannot stop. However, most people have never tried to decide when to worry or ruminate and when not to do so. They may have tried to push all worrying thoughts out of their mind, but that is different from experiencing a worrying thought and then deciding not to dwell on it, and to do something else instead. Do you believe that your worrying or self-criticism is uncontrollable? Have you ever tried to control it? It is possible that the approach of this book will help you to accept your distressing 'mental events', and you could try choosing not to worry about them. It is not a habit that can be picked up overnight, but can come with time.

When a person is worrying, they are thinking about what bad things might happen in the imminent future. However, when people talk about their worries in therapy, they seem to centre around things that have happened to them in the past. For example, I asked one client of mine who was worrying that her husband might leave her after having an affair to focus on the feelings she had when she started to worry like this. She then revealed to me that the feeling she noticed was shame about how she had ended a previous marriage through an affair. She had not realised this experience might have affected why she was worrying about this happening to her in the future. The worry had helped her to suppress these feelings of shame and guilt. After expressing this memory, she no longer needed to suppress it. After talking about her past, her shift in perspective also led her to look at the differences between her present situation and the one in the past. For example, her current relationship was going much better than the one from which she had escaped. Maybe she did not need to worry as much as she had thought. Not everyone will be able to make a link between a current worry and past experiences, but when they do, the effects are often beneficial.

Another idea about worry and self-criticism is that it is anger towards another person that is directed towards yourself. This theory does seem to apply to some people. It may be worth thinking about whether you are actually angry at a significant person in your life, like a parent or partner. Of course, this theory doesn't mean that the solution is to shout at another person rather than yourself! But, if you are angry at another person for what they have said or done, it is probably worth thinking what you might be able to do to feel heard, deal with these feelings and help stop this situation from being so upsetting again. There are some sections in the next chapter about how you can deal with other people's reactions.

Understanding worry, self-criticism and rumination

If the above ideas felt relevant to you, then you may be able to start to understand your tendency to worry, ruminate and to criticise yourself. If you believe that these things are helpful to you, then this would prevent you from giving them up. Also, if you believe that you have no control over whether or not you worry, then this would also prevent you from giving it up. Finally, if you are going to give it up, you will need to find some things to do instead – other ways to direct your attention, like reading, sport or another pastime. Other activities to do as a replacement include the brief mindfulness relaxation technique and the self-soothing style of thinking described in chapter 3. The idea is not to suppress all negative thoughts in this way, but to notice when you have these thoughts, and then choose one of these other activities instead of engaging in long periods of worry, rumination or self-critical thinking. The cognitive therapist Adrian Wells has developed a way of treating worry and rumination using this general approach. He helps people to talk about what they believe about their worry, and to test out their beliefs about it. For example, people can test whether worry is controllable by planning to worry for one hour a day (say, from 6–7pm). If they start to worry outside this time then they are asked to postpone the worry until later. This is difficult to start with, but over time it helps people to realise they have some control over their recurrent thinking, and that it may be neither as dangerous, nor as useful, as they had previously believed.

Key points

- Nearly everyone worries to some degree.
- Some people believe that worrying or being self-critical is either harmful or uncontrollable.
- Worrying can often be a distraction from more painful feelings.
- In some forms of CBT, people can learn to control when to worry and when not to worry.

9

Dealing with the consequences of the phobia

As long as each person feels a powerful need to control other people in order to avoid being controlled oneself, conflict is inevitable.

William T. Powers

Control is never achieved when sought after directly. It is the surprising outcome of letting go.

James Arthur Ray

Learning to cope with a phobia is more than just learning to deal with the anxiety itself. Over time, the phobia creates its own impact on work, education and relationships. In this section there are some suggestions about how to manage this impact, and to begin to reverse the trend.

Knowledge is power

In reading this book, you are in a better position than most people to know about fear, anxiety and phobias. The explanations here are not just common sense but are drawn from people's personal experiences as well as from scientific theories and research. With this understanding, you can begin to work out whether other people are responding to your phobia in a helpful or an unhelpful way. Hopefully, it can also provide you with the language to talk about your experiences, and help you to be understood by others. However, this will take time and only some people will be open to listening to you right away and trying to understand what you have been through. If you understand yourself slightly better after reading this book (and others like it), you have gained a way to accept yourself and make some changes, despite what people around you can understand at the moment. Their understanding may come with time.

Dealing with people who don't understand

Fears and phobias can have a big impact on relationships and, in turn, relationships can have both good and bad impacts on the phobia. It seems as though the key factor is how well friends and family members understand what a person with a phobia is going through. Very often they do not realise that your behaviour is a direct result of what you believe is about to happen. At other times they may know what you believe but be unaware of the intense distress that a fearful person can experience. Some of the most sympathetic people can innocently do or say things that make things more difficult. For example, they may think that you need more encouragement, but this can provide even more pressure. However, you need to be understanding as well. They cannot see inside your mind. No one, other than you, can.

You may be reading this book because you are someone who is concerned about a friend or family member who has a phobia. It is common for people to ask how they can be of help. There is no simple way for friends and family members to understand what is happening for the person they want to help.

In fact, it seems that most people do not understand anxiety. This may be because the common ideas people have about how to cope – 'try harder', 'cheer yourself up' – just don't work for anxiety. So, learning to cope with anxiety is even more difficult because an anxious person may need to 'buck the trend' and start to do things and believe things that have not even occurred to other people. Nevertheless, for open-minded people, the explanations in this book may go some way towards building up their understanding. Most importantly, friends and family need to be aware of three critical pieces of information:

1. *What anxious people do makes sense when you know what they are thinking.* When an anxious person does something unusual (such as pacing around or checking things), it is because they are struggling to keep safe from their unusual bodily sensations and mental events. They are not signs of being a 'nervous wreck' or 'madness'. A supportive friend or family member may be able to listen to your experiences (a problem shared is a problem halved) without trying to deny them or belittle them.

2. *What has happened to a person in the past AND what is happening right now affect whether a person is anxious.* An anxious person's problems have often developed because their early childhood experiences have made it difficult to learn how to deal with threatening situations. All problems have their origin in the past, but equally, they are also all kept going in the present because of how people deal with their fears. So, an anxious person deserves to be understood and have past difficulties taken into consideration by other people, but on the other hand the anxious person is really the only person who is in a position to learn how to manage their anxiety better right now.

3. *People can recover from their anxiety problems given time.* Following from the above, because all anxiety problems are

kept going in the present by the way that people deal with their fears, recovery is always possible – people can change how they deal with their fears. This hope needs to be balanced by the fact that change is not an overnight experience and other people cannot rush it along. It can only go at the pace of the person who is learning to manage their anxiety.

Laura's experience of dealing with other people's reaction to her anxieties

Outsiders easily misunderstand our plight. This happens an awful lot to me and makes me quite angry especially if after I have done my best to explain how it is, they fail to grasp or understand the difficulties I face. People are very quick to judge. They exhibit the common 'pull yourself together' or 'must get on' attitudes. They think they have all the answers but they actually have little knowledge to base this on.

Janet's experience of dealing with other people's reaction to her phobia

For many years, I never told anyone about my panics because I felt stupid, a failure, like a child – when I was actually a grown woman with two children! Because of this, no one could understand what was wrong with me, and so they were not supportive. Therefore their attitude towards me confirmed to me that I was stupid and a failure. Actually they just didn't understand what was going on for me. One day, in a conversation with relatives about taking one of my long routes (to avoid the traffic lights), I just came out with it. I said: 'I can't do that! I have panic attacks!' The shock on their faces when I suddenly came out with it! But I wasn't ashamed any more: 'That's how I feel, so don't ask me to do something I don't feel comfortable about.' I felt better just saying this.

Sometimes it can be difficult to put into words what you want to say about your anxiety and how to cope with it. You could try using the explanation below, either word-for-word, or changing a few details so that you are happy with it. It is designed to address the key misunderstandings that other people have and allow them to choose whether to opt in or out of your approach at this stage:

> As you know, I have a problem with anxiety. After reading about it, I have realised that there are a few facts about anxiety that I need to explain to you – it would be helpful to me if you could understand them too. The first fact is that anxiety has real physical effects on a person's body that make it difficult for them to do what they want to do. It is not just 'all in the mind'. Second, a major problem is that anxiety is made worse by pushing a person too hard, criticising them, and even encouraging them to set goals that they can't achieve. These methods just don't work. Third, the positive thing is that many people do get better or recover from their anxiety problems over a period of months or years. It seems as though the way to recover is by understanding the anxiety better, what keeps it going, and starting to deal with situations that trigger it differently. I am working on this at the moment, but I do need to try to do it at my own pace. This is the way that seems to help other people. Does this way of approaching my anxiety sound reasonable to you? If not, I can find some information for you that may answer your questions. If it does seem reasonable, are you willing to work with me on learning to cope with my anxiety?

Dealing with people who are overtly critical

A poor understanding can lead to people being critical. We know that most people do not understand what makes people anxious, including most people who are anxious themselves. People tend to explain it using very simple ideas, like 'poor motivation' or 'lack of confidence'. Other people may have more extreme beliefs about anxious people, like 'he is a nervous wreck', or 'she doesn't care enough about me to get better'. Even after serious traumas, close friends and family often still believe that any 'normal' person would have got over the problem. Occasionally, people may say these things to try to deliberately hurt the anxious person (see the next section), although this is very often not the case, and it is worth thinking of other possibilities. For example, despite being unhelpful, these kinds of statements are often other people's genuine attempts to try to understand the behaviour of someone who is anxious. People may also genuinely believe that criticising someone, or drawing attention to their faults or to possible catastrophes, are effective ways of keeping them motivated in their attempts to get better – you may even partly believe this yourself. They may say things like: 'keep on your toes!' or, 'don't get complacent!' However, the evidence suggests that this kind of negative motivation does not help, and only serves to make people feel worse and worry more. The only real way to test it out is to see what happens when a person close to you does the opposite – is comfortable with you as you are, listens to your concerns, draws attention to your good progress and is happy for you. Does this make you feel more or less motivated? Does it make you worry more or less?

I mentioned earlier that phobias are caused by several factors including genes, past experiences, and one's own behaviour. This means that an individual is not to blame for having the phobia. For this reason, it is not acceptable for other people to blame or criticise you for having the phobia and for its consequences. You can provide an example of how to deal with the phobia by the kind way that you treat yourself in making small steps towards coping better (see the examples of self-soothing in chapter 3). It may sometimes be tempting to fight back and criticise other people for their faults if they criticise you for having the phobia. However, this could escalate into an all-out conflict. If you let this happen, you are letting the phobia win. Do you really want this to happen? If a person close to you is criticising you for having the phobia, it probably shows that they don't really understand what a phobia is and what causes it. They need to learn, and you are in a position to explain it to them. Many people will be open to learning if you explain it to them in a respectful, straightforward way. If they continue to refuse to listen to you and criticise you, are they really worth your time at the moment? It may be more helpful to spend your time talking to a person who is open to learning and shows consideration.

There are some specific techniques for dealing with criticism from other people. One of these is provided by the cognitive therapist, David Burns. In the instant, you can deal with criticism by asking your criticiser to be specific, to clarify what he or she is trying to say. This is because specific criticism can be useful and true, whereas general, extreme criticism is never useful and never true. For example, 'You didn't make it to dinner' is reminding you of something that may be true, whereas, 'You can never do anything I ask you because you are so selfish' is clearly too general to be true. Asking people to be more specific also catches them off guard – you are neither accepting nor denying their criticism and you are not escalating the situation with your own attacks. You are standing your ground and asking them to refine their use of language. You don't have to accept extreme criticism that is unfounded, but you can show your strength to accept comments that may be a true reflection of events and may have led to frustration or disappointment for other people. You can even turn helpful criticism to your own advantage and see it as a useful tip or something else you can try out. Have a look at the self-soothing ways of thinking at the end of chapter 3, and the words in appendix 4. They provide more constructive ways of thinking about your difficulties and words to describe them.

Dealing with people who are abusive

Sometimes other people respond to a fearful person in ways that are more than being critical; ways that are inappropriate, manipulative or abusive. Bullies who are in a position of power often pick on people who they think will be afraid of them, knowing that they can get away with it. If you have been subjected to this kind of attack, it is very understandable to feel frustrated and angry towards these individuals. There can be a strong desire to retaliate or take revenge. These are all normal feelings given the situation. However, there may be genuine risks if you lash out or retaliate in a peak of emotion without thinking of the consequences. Your feeling of anger is completely normal, but how you deal with this feeling and how you behave towards other people when you feel this way is up to you. You may wish to think about how you can plan a way of dealing with the situation that serves two goals: to keep yourself safe and to seek justice for what has occurred. This may take time and consideration, and may involve gaining the understanding and help of other people. In some cases it may be possible to eventually repair the relationship with the abusive individual, although this is not always possible. There are relevant self-help books listed in the reading list if you feel that this situation applies to you.

Work colleagues and employers

For most people managing work or returning to work or education is a key sign of whether they are coping with their anxieties. All of the above points apply to work situations as well as to friends and family. However, there are some specific points to be considered:

1. *Anxiety disorders are common.* Anxiety and depression are often called the 'common cold' of mental health problems.

Employers should expect that a sizeable proportion of their workforce will have a significant problem with anxiety. Therefore, these difficulties should be handled in the same way as other physical health problems requiring time off or medical appointments.

2. *Disclosure.* The question of whether to disclose an anxiety condition, and who to tell is a difficult one. The important thing to remember is that the choice is yours. It is not necessarily a simple decision and you should consider the pros and cons of disclosure carefully.

3. *Applying for a job.* When applying for a job, it may be worth trying to find out the organisation's policy regarding mental health problems through other sources so that you can consider whether to disclose or not. You may feel that the job is within your abilities anyway, despite your anxiety problems, in which case it may not be helpful to tell your employer. Although it is illegal to discriminate against someone solely because they have a 'disability', there may be a worry that disclosing your anxiety problems could cause the employer to show a subtle prejudice. On the other hand, if you are concerned about carrying out the job and you would like your employers to make concessions for you (see point 4 below), then you will need to tell them about it.

4. *Flexible work practices.* If you choose to disclose an anxiety condition then it is good practice for your employers to make reasonable changes to your work practice. Indeed, if your anxiety problems constitute a significant 'disability' then under the 1995 Disability Discrimination Act, your employer is legally obliged to make 'reasonable adjustments' to your conditions for work. An example might be having time off each week to see a psychologist, or changing your office routine in a way that is less stressful for you. However, the meaning of 'reasonable' varies widely between different industries and different employers. If your

employer can understand that a more flexible work practice could help you cope better, then they may realise that it is often in their interests too. Maybe you could suggest it to them for a trial period of a few months to see whether it is beneficial for you and the company. Alternatively, you may consider seeking advice first from an organisation such as No Panic or MIND (contact details are in appendix 6).

Key points

As you understand your phobia better, you can begin to work out who is responding to your problems in a helpful way.

- A supportive friend or family member may be able to listen to your experiences without trying to deny them or belittle them.
- Because phobias are caused by several factors no one person can be completely to blame for causing a phobia.
- Your employers may find out that being more flexible for people with anxiety problems can be in their own interests.

10

I am still not coping with my phobia. Why not?

Our greatest glory is not in never failing, but in rising up every time we fail.

Ralph Waldo Emerson

Every act of conscious learning requires the willingness to suffer an injury to one's self-esteem. That is why young children, before they are aware of their own self-importance, learn so easily.

Thomas Szasz

By the time you have reached this point in the book, you are still likely to have problems with your anxiety. This section focuses on some of the main reasons behind people feeling that they are still not coping, and so getting frustrated with their progress.

Common 'road blocks' to coping, and how to deal with them

Below I have tried to cover the most common obstacles that arise when people try to put their plan for coping into action. I have provided answers to these questions, further points to consider, and references to sections of the book that might help.

Why didn't I get help like this earlier?

Before even starting on a self-help programme, it is normal to think something like, 'Well if this really is it – the cure – then why didn't I get help earlier?' You may think this and feel angry at people, at whoever must have denied you this help in the past. You could spend your time thinking about this, going over how you could have got help in the past, feeling annoyed at past missed opportunities. You could use these feelings to distract you from actually helping yourself now, from taking the responsibility and time to read this book and put it into practice. You could do that. Would it be helpful to you? Alternatively, you could accept that your feelings of anger are partly justified, and yet try out this programme anyway, for your own good. You can only live your life in the present and make what future you have now. You cannot change the past, nor will postponing your plans to a vague time in the future help you right now.

I must be able to explain all my symptoms.

This book has tried to explain how some unusual experiences, like feelings of unreality and numbness, can develop from vicious cycles of feelings, thoughts, behaviours and their physical effects. However, there may be experiences you have had that are not explained here. It would be tempting to think, 'Unless the ideas in this book can explain all my symptoms, then it's not worth trying to cope with any of them.' But it is possible that some of your symptoms are a direct cause of a physical problem unrelated to anxiety. So it may be a good idea to focus on the symptoms that could be a result of anxiety first, rather than focusing on the experiences that do not fit. There may not be an explanation for everything we experience, and part of coping is about learning to accept this uncertainty.

I'm not progressing quickly enough!

This is a very common frustration – once we have made the decision to make changes and deal with our problems, we want them to be fixed straight away. This is easier when we understand exactly what the problem is – a broken pencil can be replaced; a leaky roof can be repaired by a builder. The problem with the causes of anxiety is that they are different for each of us, and the anxious person is in the best position to understand their own anxiety, not other people. Most of us have had pretty long, complicated lives, and so making changes to our habits and our beliefs takes time. It is like untangling a knotted ball of wool. We might apply a few simple techniques to do this: look for the ends, feed the end back through the knots, roll up the untangled strands carefully; but these techniques need to be applied over time, to every tangle of wool, to each troubled event that comes up in a person's life. The idea is that you work through this gradually, but it takes time and patience to unroll and tidy the strands of your life.

My progress is not good enough!

A very immediate response to not coping is to want to criticise yourself or other people. Somebody must be to blame for me not coping! If it's not me then it's my mother, my partner, my boss or my friends! It is of course possible that you or other people may have done something that made it difficult to cope this time. Fair enough. What is the next step? To tell yourself that you are stupid for not getting it right this time, or to try to understand what happened so it can be avoided next time? If you have noticed that you are being very critical of yourself or other people in this way, then this is a step. Now you can decide whether you want to continue being critical, or whether you want to put your time into trying to understand the situation. You may want to consider alternative ways of talking to your self, like the self-soothing statements in chapter 3. Appendix 4 also provides some examples of the kinds of words and phrases that are helpful for people learning to cope, and those that are not. For example, using words like 'should' and 'must' seems to make people more stressed than using words like 'can' and 'could', so, it is better to think 'I can get over this!' rather than 'I must get over this!'

Reading the book doesn't make a difference!

Books are only words. Unlike people, they don't respond to you, and you don't have to answer to them. I am not going to know whether you put any of the ideas in this book into practice or not. Reading this book (or any book for that matter) is not enough to help a person, although trying out some of the ideas in it for yourself may be enough. Is it possible that you could be focusing on the elements of the book that do not fit with your experiences as a way of distracting yourself from getting started on what might work and trying some of the ideas out? Part of learning to cope may be to focus on the parts of the book that might work, to imagine trying these things out in your head, and then to try doing them in real life. Go on ... do it.

I must challenge myself more!

An important part of chapter 7 was the idea of setting small, achievable goals and working through them gradually. It is worth asking yourself whether the goals you have set are achievable. If not, then try to think of a way of breaking them down, making them simpler, as your first step. If there is something that makes the situation worse, is there a way to face the situation without that? For example, if going to a supermarket is your goal, could you start on a quiet morning during the week? The next step could be a time that is slightly more busy. However, you do not need to make another step if the current step already makes you anxious. You can stick with it for a while before moving up. Of course you will need to appreciate that no situation can be completely controlled, and partly what you are learning is to accept that there is uncertainty in every situation, and to manage these changes if you need to.

An example of how Alice created achievable goals

> I wanted to cope with the anxiety I felt when I drove to the shops in my local town. I broke the journey down into small stages. I practised just driving through the traffic lights and then returning home. I soon realised that they could not trap me against my will as I had imagined. When I first tackled the High Street, I set what turned out to be an unachievable goal at that time. I became extremely anxious and suffered a setback. In the past I would have convinced myself that the High Street was now impossible. But this time I decided to break it down into three stages and I have now managed those successfully. My next stage is to try to leave my car and buy a parking ticket.

I am still getting anxious!

People's frustration with learning to cope often boils down to this – they are still feeling anxious. For this problem, there are a few things to consider again:

1. *Removing anxious feelings is not your goal.* Learning to cope with anxiety is not learning to eliminate anxiety. The aim of this programme is not to remove all unpleasant feelings. So, you will still feel anxious even once you have made some progress. We are not measuring your progress by how anxious you feel, but by what you have actually done, despite your anxiety.

2. *Are you waiting long enough?* Chapter 4 explained that feelings of anxiety drop with time, as long as the person does not
   encounter or think about further things that may frighten
   them. So, if you stay with the physical sensations and don't
   try to control them, they go away by themselves. This is
   because the adrenaline in your bloodstream that causes the
   sensations is broken down within several minutes.
   However, the irony is that you need to let go of trying to control these sensations for them to go down. So, providing you
   are letting go, the longer you spend in a situation, the less
   anxious you will feel. This is especially true if the situation is
   quite static and unchanging, such as looking at a photo of
   what you are afraid of, but it can work for real situations too.

3. *Have you dropped your 'safety behaviours'?* Chapter 5
   explained how the things that we do to try to make ourselves
   feel safe can often make things worse. For example, trying
   not to look shaky by tensing your muscles can make you feel
   more tense and controlled. Are there any safety behaviours
   that you may still be using? Do they work? Is it possible they
   might be making your sensations of anxiety more intense? If
   your safety behaviours don't always work and might make
   you feel worse, could it be time to try facing the same situation without them?

4. *Is worrying interfering with your concentration?* Chapter 8
   covers worry and other forms of 'recurrent thinking'.
   Focusing on worrying thoughts can make it particularly difficult to get used to a feared situation. When we worry over
   things it takes our attention away from what is really happening; it can also lead us to think of other frightening
   things, that in turn leads to another squirt of adrenaline in
   our bloodstream – causing the feelings of anxiety to continue. If worry seems to be your main problem, return to
   chapter 8 and read about some alternative coping strategies.
   Worry and safety behaviours are usually the most likely

reasons for anxiety staying high, rather than any physical difference between you and other people

5. *Have you worked out what you are really afraid of happening?* Part of the ten-step plan involves trying to state what you think might happen if you face a feared situation. Sometimes this can be difficult to put into words. Often we find ourselves trying to escape upsetting or frightening feelings without really thinking why we are doing it. By reminding ourselves of the worst fear before going into the situation, we are making sure that each time facing the situation is a test of whether or not the worst case scenario will happen. So, if your prediction was 'I will get very anxious' then try to think beyond this – we already know that you are likely to feel anxious. What is it about the feelings of anxiety that make them so awful? Are you worried about the physical effects like a life-threatening illness, or about what other people will do when you feel this way? The prediction: 'I will get so anxious that other people will abandon me' is a more extreme belief that can be tested out. You could also look for evidence for the alternative belief: 'I will get anxious but other people will deal with it OK.' 'I will feel so short of breath that I will suffocate and die' is another example of an extreme belief, in this case you could consider the alternative: 'I will feel short of breath but I will still take in enough air to be OK.' This allows you to feel nervous, and to focus on whether this has the impact you had imagined, or whether you can cope despite it.

6. *Is this 'normal' fear?* If the situation you are facing is one that would make most people nervous, then maybe you are experiencing normal fear. Examples are public speaking and walking in areas that are known crime spots. One way to find out would be to ask other people whether they might feel nervous in this situation or not. They might cope with their anxiety differently and you could learn how they manage it.

My anxiety is not about what I 'believe' – it's just a really unbearable physical feeling.

Some people say that their feelings of anxiety can sometimes be so extreme that it is unbearable and indescribable – a feeling of extreme impending doom that is hard to put into words. It would be very difficult for people who experience normal fear but have never had serious problems with anxiety to really understand this feeling. There may be times when you experience feelings like this. I can suggest some possible ways of coping with this experience. The first one is to ask yourself whether you need to put yourself in a situation that leads to this extreme feeling right now. After all, the plan for the book is to take things gradually and start with moderate amounts of anxiety, not overwhelming amounts. Could you set a goal that is more manageable? Also, you may believe that you might feel like this even in quite a mild situation. Could this be something you could test out? Maybe this extreme feeling doesn't occur every time – and by trying out different, less challenging, situations, you can see whether it does or not. However, sometimes it may be difficult to avoid situations that make you feel this way. If so, try to think 'What am I actually afraid might happen?' OK, it feels unbearable, so what if you were not able to bear the feeling? What awful thing would happen to you? Can you test whether this occurs or not? Finally, look at step 6 of the ten-step plan – there is some information there about dealing with 'peaks' of anxiety. It may seem that you need to do something to cope with unbearable feelings of anxiety. What would happen if you did nothing but just notice the feeling? There may come a time when you wish to test this out.

There is a serious reason why I am anxious.

Some people may have problems with their anxiety, and be in a situation that would make anyone very stressed and upset. For example, they may have had a recent bereavement or they may be suffering from a chronic terminal illness. If you are in this unfortunate situation, then your loss needs to be acknowledged. You are suffering at the moment and this is an even stronger reason for being kind to yourself. If you are worrying about the consequences, then you may find it helpful to return to chapter 8. You may consider whether there is someone who can talk to you and listen to your experience without judging you or interfering, such as a counsellor, therapist or other kind, supportive figure (see chapter 12). The staff on national helplines are also well trained for this purpose (see appendix 6 for details). Some people find it helpful to write about their difficulties – and studies show that this can help people to cope with traumatic experiences. Part of learning to deal with real adversity is knowing what you need to accept as being out of your control, and what you can do, despite the problems. Chapter 11 focuses on this approach. Many people do learn to cope better even when they have had a recent loss or there are very major current problems in their lives.

I cannot even face my darkest thoughts because they are so unbearable.

Some people may feel that their deepest, most threatening thoughts can never be tested out. The person may not even accept that they have them, and try to suppress them whenever they appear. These might be thoughts of something wicked or immoral, like hitting someone or abusing them in some way, or fears that are so catastrophic that experiencing them seems unbearable. It may take great courage even to acknowledge them. One way to think about this obstacle is to think about what power a thought can actually have. Can a thought about doing a bad thing really mean that you are a bad person? Does keeping the thought of something extremely frightening in your mind actually make it happen? One study (Rachman & de Silva, 1978), found that the vast majority of people get disturbing thoughts of this kind. However, only people with 'disorders' were preoccupied and distressed by them. Somehow, most people seem to be able to let go of thoughts of this kind. They don't judge themselves for the thought they have had. For example, do you think that Stephen King, the famous horror author, is an evil man? He has never committed a crime and leads a happy life. Yet he must allow the most morbid thoughts to go through his mind so that he can write those graphic novels. What makes anyone else different?

I feel guilty – it is not acceptable for me to get better.

Often, when a person starts to get better, they feel guilty. There is often a very good reason for this. For example, if a person has experienced a serious trauma which led other people to suffer much more, it may not seem right to get better, when other people are still suffering. These feelings of guilt can be a very difficult obstacle to recovery. Sometimes, people may be able to combine helping themselves with also helping others, so that this difference is reduced. When another person has died, then recovery depends on beginning to accept the loss, mourning the other person fully and with compassion, and reaching a point where the loss is acknowledged and understood. So, for some people, coping with anxiety is also a struggle to cope with loss and becoming less anxious goes in tandem with gradually accepting what has happened. Sometimes, trying to see oneself from the perspective of the other person can help. Would they want me to suffer in this way? How could I respond in a way that would do justice to them? How could I help prevent this from happening to someone else in the future? Often, meeting with people who have been through similar experiences and come out the other end and are managing well, can be very helpful.

Everything going on in my life is too overwhelming at the moment.

There are periods of extreme distress when it is hard to cope with anxiety by yourself, or using a self-help book. A self-help book relies on you having times when you can sit, read, take in and consider what is written. During extreme distress this is not possible. If you are experiencing constant anxiety or are in severe panic every day then it would be advisable for you to access more immediate help. Similarly if you have severe depression or are having frequent thoughts of suicide, this is not a time to be using a guide, and you need more immediate help. In the first instance, see your GP, care worker if you have one, or if they are unavailable, go to the accident and emergency section of your local hospital. National emergency helplines are listed in appendix 6.

Other people have not acknowledged what I have achieved!

Often other people do not recognise the gradual gains that you can make during a programme of this kind. It can be very frustrating. However, try thinking about your progress from other people's perspective. Could they always notice the subtle changes you are making to things, like what you focus your attention on, and whether or not you are using a discreet safety behaviour (like tensing your muscles)? If other people are being overtly critical of your progress, take another look at chapter 9 to see how to respond. Sometimes other people may suggest you approach your problems in ways that don't fit with the approach of this book (such as, 'You just need to really push yourself!'). They have a right to make suggestions, and you may decide to try them out. However, they may be suggesting you do something that you have already tried and that didn't help. If so, this can be frustrating, but try to remember that they may be trying to help and without seeing into your mind (which is impossible, even for a therapist!) they can't be expected to come up with exactly the right advice for you.

Key points

- It takes time to learn to cope with anxiety.
- You will still feel anxious even when you have made some progress.
- If you stay with feelings of anxiety, and don't try to control them, they can drop eventually.
- Part of learning to cope involves putting what you have read into practice.

11

Living a valued life

Grant me the serenity to accept the things I cannot change, the courage to change the things I can, and the wisdom to know the difference.

Saint Francis of Assisi

Courage is not the absence of fear, but rather the judgement that something else is more important than fear.

Ambrose Redmoon

People often say that this or that person has not yet found himself. But the self is not something one finds, it is something one creates.

Thomas Szasz

This chapter is designed to draw together what I have written in the previous chapters into a single philosophy, or approach to life. In essence, I think the key themes of the book are as follows:

1. There are some things that we have very little control over.
2. There are some things that we have a lot of control over.

3. We can move forward in life by making the choices that best suit our needs in the areas we can control, and accepting the things we can't and letting go of them. We can get better at this over time.

Point 1 may seem pessimistic at first. Why is it useful to know that there are things that we have very little control over? There could be several reasons. First, it allows us to prioritise, and focus on what we can control rather than wasting time and energy trying to control things that we cannot. For example, if we cannot control our physical feelings of anxiety then we can move our attention to something more important to us, like being a good parent or friend. Second, it allows us to test out our fearful beliefs. If we let go of trying to control our feelings, we realise that they don't get out of control by themselves. Third, it allows us to realise that trying to exert control over everything that happens to us just does not work. We cannot have complete control over our thoughts, our feelings and over what other people do. More extreme attempts at control include criticism, bullying and abuse. By letting go of trying hard to control things we cannot control, we can experiment with being less perfectionist, and learn to accept uncertainty, mistakes, inner conflict and error. I think that we need to accept these at times because it is from these that we can learn new ways of dealing with things in the future. So, much of this book is about focusing on this uncertainty, because out of uncertainty, alternative ways of seeing a problem and coping with it can arise.

Building acceptance of uncertainty – Laura

> I have gradually realised over time, that life is uncertain, and I am coming to accept this. In the past, I did not realise that it was possible, leading me to spend years in turmoil and limbo. I can now say that one day I can and will accept the uncertainty of life, which is such a powerful thing to finally realise.

There are other things that we can generally control in our lives. To realise this, we need to be aware of them. The most fundamental thing we can typically control is what we focus on – what we choose to look at, listen to, smell, taste and feel. Even so, there are limits. We cannot look at a beautiful scene if it is obscured from view, or hear some quiet music if there is loud background noise. So, we can be more active in controlling some of our experiences. These include getting new information, warm clothes, tasty food, recuperating rests, pleasant journeys, fulfilling sunshine and invigorating walks. Again, some of these are limited some of the time – you might not enjoy walking in torrential rain for example! So we need to think again. What can I control, given the limits? This is the idea behind building up goals gradually. It helps to focus on what can be achieved. We don't have complete control over other people, but we can often share experiences of closeness, enjoyment, kindness and learning with other people. It is some of these things that we attempt to develop, despite those things that we cannot control. They become the strengths, skills, values and resources that we build on. At the end of this chapter is a table to record these over time.

As implied by Saint Francis of Assisi's statement, it is not always easy to know what you can control. So maybe it is best not to assume that something is completely outside your control, nor equally that you can have complete control over it. Often, when you think about a situation in detail, there is something you can do, and so over time you learn to cope more effectively as you try out these new ways of thinking and behaving. I designed the ten-step plan to make that process as systematic as possible, but you may well have your own ideas of how to go about it. You may find that as you notice your strengths, resources and values, you become more confident in trying to face the feelings of anxiety that form the basis of the ten-step plan. There is no need to run before you can walk. Your strength will build up from these early small successes at coping.

How Janet developed her strengths, resources and values

> Over time, I felt more confident. I signed up for a computer course and passed three exams. I got a job behind a bar and I was good at it (I would never have said that about myself in the past). I am now a social support worker in the community. I have to drive to places I'm not familiar with and go through numerous traffic lights. My car radio helps, and the water is still needed. I still have anxious moments but I cope. Those were very dark days in the past, and I regret not seeking help sooner. But I feel that things happen for a reason and now in my line of work I am more understanding because I know what it is like to have such poor confidence and to feel like your self-esteem just doesn't exist.

Commitment and change

As you choose to move on in your goals, you will be showing your commitment to them over time. You may choose not to keep a record of these, or you may choose to keep a diary or notes in some other format. Within this book, there are three different suggestions of ways you can record your progress. There is the table to record each time you use the ten-step plan (at the end of chapter 7), with a space for writing what you have learnt, and at the end of this chapter there is the record of experiences that reflect strengths, qualities and resources that you can copy each time you wish to use it. You may also find it helpful to produce a list of the main values you are committed to and record your commitment to them in the table below. This is a better record for the long term. Examples of values could be 'being kind to others', 'educating other people', 'having new, fulfilling experiences', 'building up my knowledge'. In the right hand column you could put examples of things you are doing that fit with these values. Finally, the scale at the end of chapter 3 ('Seven Helpful Beliefs') can be used to see how helpful beliefs you may have about yourself and other people are changing over time.

Table 11.1 My values

What do I value in life? Who is important to me? What principles do I believe in?	How am I living my life according to these values?
1.	1.
2.	2.
3.	3.
4.	4.
5.	5.

Strengths, qualities and resources

It is very easy to forget the strengths, qualities and resources that we have. This table is divided into different strengths and resources with examples of things you may do that reflect that quality. When you are going through a time when your confidence is low, it can be helpful to tick these things off as you do them. Each time you do it reflects a strength or resource that you are recovering, or developing.

Table 11.2 Strengths, qualities and resources

Caring	
I have taken care of myself in some way (e.g. bath, shower, eating nice food)	☐
I have praised myself for something I have done today	☐
I have listened to another person's problems	☐
I have helped another person with a task	☐
I have given another person some useful information or advice	☐
I have thanked someone else for something they have said or done	☐
I have looked after a plant, animal or person today	☐

Skills

I have done something round my home (e.g. cleaning, gardening, tidying, cooking) ☐

I have done something that I enjoy (e.g. reading, watching television, sport, game) ☐

I have created something that I like (e.g. drawing, painting, song, story, ornament) ☐

I have done some work, or made a step in a plan that I have ☐

Experience

I have remembered something good or enjoyable that I have done in the past ☐

I have remembered a fact or skill that will be useful to me ☐

Knowledge

I have learnt something from a book, magazine, newspaper, television or internet ☐

I have learnt something by talking to another person ☐

Communication

I have had a conversation in person or on the phone ☐

I have written a letter or email today ☐

Relationships

I have done something enjoyable with another person ☐

I have worked on something with another person ☐

I have laughed about something with another person ☐

Coping

I have done something that I want to do, despite my feelings of anxiety ☐

I have done what I can in a situation, and been pleased with what I have managed ☐

I have been honest with myself about how I feel ☐

I have taken a step back from a difficult situation and reacted differently from usual ☐

The table of strengths, qualities and resources is available online.

Key points

- It helps to realise that there are some things that we have little control over.
- It helps to focus on what you *can* control in your life.
- It helps to notice uncertainties, mistakes and conflicts so that new ways of thinking about a problem and dealing with it can come to mind.
- As we build on what we can control, and let go of what we cannot, we can live our lives according to our chosen values, by drawing on our strengths, qualities and resources.

12

Treatments for phobias and anxiety disorders – professional help

Formerly, when religion was strong and science weak, men mistook magic for medicine; now, when science is strong and religion weak, men mistake medicine for magic.

Thomas Szasz

There is no medicine like hope, no incentive so great, and no tonic so powerful as expectation of something tomorrow.

Orison Swett Marden

Many people with anxiety problems will have already sought help of one form or another. And while you are reading this book, it may be helpful to be seeking treatment more directly. However, the quality of help available varies widely. A simple rule seems to be that no one source of help provides all that you need, but you can often get something helpful from each one. It is probably best to shop around. You want what works for you, and so if you buy completely into one person's approach, it is unlikely to suit you in every way. Here are some ideas to consider when researching possible sources of professional help.

Support groups

Beyond self-help guides of this kind (and there are others listed in the reading list in appendix 5), the next best stop is probably a support group. They are good because they are used to having members with mixed views, and tend to encourage discussion and debate. Many actually have treatment programmes available, occasionally individually, and sometimes in local groups or on the phone. The most well-known national groups are listed in appendix 6, but you may find that a local independent group is available.

National guidelines

Before focusing on what is actually available from your local medical services, I would like to show you what the *ideal* is, which is far from what is universally available. NICE is the National Institute for Health and Clinical Excellence – their contact details are in appendix 6. It recruits groups of experts to recommend the best treatments for different health problems. There are treatment guidelines for many different anxiety problems available to download on their website. They tend to recommend CBT or related psychological therapies, often over and above drug treatments. However, there are too few psychological specialists available to deliver these recommended treatments. It is a frustrating aspect of the health service, but one that is likely to improve in the long term.

The medical profession

For many people, their GP will be the first person they have told about their fears and phobias in detail. GPs provide a valuable first point of contact for people with anxiety problems, and they can prescribe medication for short-term alleviation of symptoms. For more serious mental health problems like severe depression, medication is usually offered as the main long-term treatment, and problems with anxiety are often not considered for separate treatment. People with more severe problems are usually referred to psychiatrists (doctors who specialise in mental health problems) and meet regularly with care-coordinators who are often mental health nurses or social workers. Most doctors are aware that long-term treatment for anxiety problems requires a psychological therapy or a self-help programme and many are frustrated with the lack of resources which can limit their ability to refer patients for therapy.

Some members of the medical profession may be less aware of the evidence for psychological treatments for anxiety, or may have rather fixed views about people's capacity for change. This can give patients an overly pessimistic view of their situation, or put them into conflict with their doctor. If this applies to you, then you may want to think about whether an alternative doctor is available or you may wish to join a group of local service users who have similar concerns about their services.

It is understandable that people who are specialists in certain fields will believe that problems have their cause in an area within which they are an expert. However, they are probably not as well acquainted with other areas of expertise, so keep an open mind if you are given the impression by a medical professional that the cause of your problems is simple, or permanent. What is more important is how you can help yourself now, rather than what the root cause of your problems was.

Cognitive Behavioural Therapy (CBT)

CBT is the main form of therapy available and so it may be helpful for me to spend some time explaining what you might expect if you are interested in having a course of this therapy. Cognitive therapy was developed by Aaron T. Beck in the 1950s and 60s, and in the 1970s and 80s merged with the field of behaviour therapy to form CBT. There are now many forms of CBT practiced by different health professionals, and it is continually evolving. Nevertheless, you will probably recognise some of the ideas covered in this book, from the description of CBT below.

CBT involves good teamwork between the therapist and client. They work together to try to understand the client's difficulties and what may influence them. The therapist can be regarded as an expert on CBT whereas the client is an expert on his or her own life and experiences. Both are vital to understanding the problem. To work out the solution to a problem, it helps to know where you are going. So, the therapist and client agree on the goals of the therapy early on. They try to set a small number of goals that are measurable, realistic and achievable. Big tasks are broken down into small steps, leading to small victories on the way to recovery.

The therapy is focused mainly on present issues, but it often visits the past to inform the present – to help understand how the client's current problems may have developed. The client's own explanation is the starting point. CBT sessions are typically 50 minutes in length and usually weekly, but this is open to discussion. Part of working as a team is that both people know what is happening. So, at the start of the session, the therapist and client agree on a plan for how to use the time. Sometimes it is useful to involve family members, friends and other health professionals in CBT.

CBT does not teach people to 'think positively'. Nor does it teach people how to completely eliminate all distress. Instead, CBT encourages 'balanced' thinking. It helps people to notice their surroundings, their own thoughts and feelings, and the relationship between them. From here they can work out ways of seeing the world and dealing with it that are more helpful to them. In everyday life things can all seem to happen at once. CBT helps to disentangle experiences, making them easier to understand. With the help of the client, the therapist works out a psychological map (sometimes called a formulation or a model), which is a joint understanding of the client's problems and what may contribute to them. The map usually contains thoughts, moods, behaviours, bodily changes and aspects of the environment (which includes other people's behaviour).

CBT is time-limited. The client is typically offered a fixed, but negotiable, number of sessions, often between ten and twenty, but sometimes more. The therapy is designed to help prevent future problems. So, towards the end, the therapist and client work together to produce a 'blueprint' of what they have covered, and a plan of how to cope with difficulties that may arise in the future. CBT aims to help people use their own existing strengths, and develop further strengths, so that they can face future problems without the help of therapy.

Rasheeda's experience of CBT

In the course of the CBT I undertook, my therapist and I created a map of my thoughts, feelings and behaviours when encountering a spider at home. Before my therapy I always focused on my feelings when encountering a spider; I crucially also believed that my behaviours were helping me cope with these feelings. Most of these behaviours however were doing the exact opposite, they were helping to maintain my fear. For example by staying away from the spider, pacing up and down my house and thinking up plans of how to get rid of it I only managed to increase my anxiety. By avoiding looking at it, I never found out that if I did look at it for a bit longer my anxiety would naturally diminish as adrenaline levels decreased. And most importantly by finding someone else to get rid of it I confirmed my thought that I couldn't cope and never found out that I actually could. I also learnt a great deal about how my behaviours affected the way I thought and felt about my experience. For example the fact that I took many deep breaths gave me the feeling of

Continued

hyperventilating and made me feel more anxious. Also, coming back to the room to check and recheck what the spider was up to confirmed my thought that the spider would ruin my day and my sleep.

As a result of identifying all these behaviours we managed to make a list of behaviours and thoughts that would be helpful. Such as imagining the spider move so that I am better prepared to cope with my anxiety when it actually does, and also focusing on the spider and its surroundings and staying with the feeling until the anxiety lessens.

My anxiety has reduced considerably since I had CBT and this map was a big part of it.

Accessing CBT

CBT in the UK is more readily available on the National Health Service than it is from private services. However, you can also access private therapists, for example by contacting BABCP (which also lists NHS therapists – see appendix 6). Typically, people ask their GP or other medical professional for a referral to see a CBT therapist. Given that CBT is recommended as the first line treatment for anxiety problems, there should be no problem in joining a waiting list. However, depending on your local service, you may have to wait many months. It can seem pointless to join a waiting list that is six months long, and it is certainly nowhere near ideal practice. However, by joining a waiting list you are making your local NHS aware of the demand for CBT. And in the context of how long you may have already been suffering from your phobia, even a wait of six months may be worthwhile. The earlier you can get on the list, the earlier you will receive the appropriate help. Remember, CBT can vary according to the therapist and their style of working, and so even if you have had an unsuccessful course of CBT in the past, it may work out to try a new course with a different therapist.

Other psychological treatments

Most psychological treatments offered through your health service will be evidence-based, that is they work for many people. So, even if you cannot access CBT, you may find other forms of therapy helpful. They include behaviour therapy, family therapy, cognitive analytical therapy, and some forms of psychodynamic therapy. It is important that your therapist can name the kind of therapy you will be offered, and that they can explain to you how what you are working on with the therapist fits the description of the therapy. Once you have a name for the therapy you are being offered, you may want to read more about it yourself. If it is CBT, the therapist should be able to explain how what you are working on together fits the principles of CBT covered in this book. In some locations you may be offered counselling. Again, while this may not be an active treatment, you may be pleasantly surprised and find it useful.

Choosing whether to start medication

I am not an expert on medication, so I will leave the details to a minimum. More details are available from the books, websites and service user groups listed at the end of the book. There are many different forms of medication that you might be offered, each to deal with different kinds of symptoms. Yet there are general principles that you could consider:

1. *Am I fully informed about this medication?* If you are considering taking a substance that will alter your state of mind, you will want to make an informed choice. You might want to ask:

   • Is this the recommended treatment for my problems, or am I missing out on the first line treatment? As the first line treatment for anxiety problems and mild depression is typically a psychological treatment, it is quite likely that medication is not the ideal treatment. Nevertheless many people find it helpful. Even if the first line treatment is not available, it is important to be aware of this.

- What is the purpose of this medication? To help with sleep, reduce anxiety, relieve symptoms of depression?
- How long will the course be? You are likely to want to be prepared for coming off the medication eventually. In relation to this, you may want to find out what the withdrawal symptoms are. Often these are actually the return of the anxiety symptoms.
- What are the possible side effects of this medication? This is a difficult question to answer because different people have different side effects, which leads to a huge list on the drug package, even though most people will not experience most of the side effects that are listed. However, some drugs do have common side effects, like weight gain, that are worth knowing about.

2. *What are the pros and cons of taking this course of medication?* With the above information, you can make a decision about whether you want to try taking the medication. You could write a list of the possible advantages and disadvantages to try to weigh them up. One option is to try out a course to see how it goes. You are the person who is the final judge on whether the medication is working. Do you notice improvements after starting the medication? Another idea is to try some other ways of coping first, like those in the book, and then come back to medication if they don't seem to work.

3. *Be prepared to take the medication as indicated.* If you take the medication as prescribed then you will have a good test of whether it works for you. However, if you don't take it as indicated, or stop and start the medication, it will be difficult to know whether it would have worked. You should also be

aware that stopping and starting medication could lead to other changes in your body that you may notice.

4 *The placebo effect.* A proportion of people get better when given tablets even if they don't contain any active medication. This is worth remembering if you respond well to medication. Partly this could be down to the drug, and partly it could be down to your own faith in it working. In fact, there is evidence that the belief in a placebo working can have direct chemical effects on the brain that lead to improvements in people's symptoms. Some studies have found an increased release of the mood-enhancing brain chemical, dopamine, in people 'treated' with a placebo – this is another example of the mind-body link described earlier in the book.

5. *Anxiolytic medication (tranquillisers).* People with anxiety problems may be offered medication to deal with poor sleep or to deal with symptoms of depression. In most cases these treatments seem not to interfere with psychological treatment. However, there is evidence that medication that directly removes the symptoms of anxiety (for example, benzodiazepines) actually make it more difficult for people to recover from the anxiety problems in the long-term. Because of this evidence, anxiolytic medication is no longer a recommended treatment for anxiety disorders. So, if your doctor offers you something to remove your anxiety, ask him or her whether the medication belongs to this group of drugs. Many people were prescribed these medications many years ago and are still taking them. See the section below for information on coming off medication.

6. *Tolerating anxiety.* Many people with anxiety problems who take medication want their feelings of anxiety to be reduced, or eliminated completely. In this respect, medication is a form of 'safety behaviour'. Safety behaviours are very understandable, and can be a useful bridge to coping better in the long term. However, we have established that learning

to cope seems partly to be about facing these feelings and learning to tolerate them. If you can still attempt to do this while you are taking medication, then the coping strategies may be just as helpful.

Coming off medication

People can have many good reasons for wanting to come off their medication, including increasing independence, side effects, and a desire to continue to cope better. For some people it comes naturally when they start to face their feelings of anxiety – the opposite of what they were trying to do when they started the medication. One way of thinking about coming off a long-term medication is that it is like dropping a safety behaviour or facing a new anxiety-provoking situation. This is because the most common withdrawal symptoms are the return of the anxiety symptoms themselves. This means that it is a difficult process. So, you may want to approach coming off medication in the same, gradual, systematic way as when you are doing the ten-step plan. Indeed, it may be sufficient to face the same situations as before, but after reducing the medication by a small amount. This is a step in itself. Then, when you have completed the plan for that level of medication, and when you are ready to move on, use the next drop as the following step. Note that you do not need to challenge yourself in any other ways during this time – reducing the medication is enough of a challenge. Just as in the ten-step plan, a small step is ideal, so you may need to work out a way of reducing your medication by small increments over a long period. Your prescriber should be happy to work on this with you, especially if they can see that you have a clear plan. It is up to you whether you want to reduce your medication. To help make up your mind, you could list the pros and cons of coming off your medication, considering some of the issues about medication noted earlier.

Key points

- Support groups provide a good source of information and some provide treatment.
- National guidelines propose psychological therapy (mainly CBT) as the first line treatment for anxiety problems.
- CBT is a short-term therapy where the therapist and client work together to try to understand what is keeping the anxiety going and to develop better ways to cope with it.
- It can be worth joining a waiting list to get CBT.
- Other psychological treatments, including counselling, may be helpful.
- Try to get the information you need to decide whether to try medication.
- Coming off medication is a gradual process like facing a new anxiety-provoking situation.

13

The last word

Every day you may make progress. Every step may be fruitful. Yet there will stretch out before you an ever-lengthening, ever-ascending, ever-improving path. You know you will never get to the end of the journey. But this, so far from discouraging, only adds to the joy and glory of the climb.

Sir Winston Churchill

For my part I know nothing with any certainty, but the sight of the stars makes me dream.

Vincent Van Gogh

Phew! You've got to the end!

I expect that even though you have got to this point in the book (or are taking a sneaky peak early on), that you are still in a position of conflict, of uncertainty. Part of you thinks that the book is helpful. But I would guess that part of you thinks that the book is not quite as helpful as it could be, because you might be different, that what it says here doesn't quite fit with your own personal fears.

If you are in this state of mind, then that is a good state of mind to be in – partly optimistic, partly sceptical. You are right if you think that the book doesn't exactly explain your predicament – you are unique. Everyone's fears are different in some ways. However, if you can find the parts of the book that do fit, the experiences that you do share with others, then you are beginning to make use of the book, to see how you can cope better like others have. It will take some time. Or it might prompt you to look elsewhere for what works for you (chapter 12 provides some ideas).

I hope that whatever your state of uncertainty, the book has led you to consider a few things: that you are not alone in suffering from anxiety; that your problems are real yet it is possible to understand some of them better; that you can start to question certain beliefs that you may have held for a long time; and that you can have some hope and optimism for the future, despite the setbacks that there may be on the way.

I wish you all the best. The next stage is all up to you!

Appendices

The material in the appendices, along with other tables from the book and further information are also available in electronic form from the website:

www.oneworld-publications.com/fears

Appendix 1

A graded introduction to the symptoms of phobias

Below are some experiences that people have when they are stressed, anxious or fearful. All of them are common during stress and are not a sign of personal weakness, or mental or physical illness in themselves. However, they can often feel very frightening when first experienced because they are so unusual and sometimes very vivid. Fortunately they are all temporary and reduce in intensity after a while or during times of less stress.

Have you sometimes noticed these feelings when you haven't been anxious?

Following are some possible explanations for experiences that many people report when feeling anxious or fearful.

Heart Racing

An efficient, healthy heart beats faster and stronger when it needs to.

When you think of something dangerous, your body secretes adrenaline which increases your heart rate. This prepares you for 'fight or flight'. Were you thinking of something frightening just before you noticed your heart race?

When you become more physically active, your heart rate increases to send more oxygen to your muscles. Did you exert yourself in some way?

Certain chemicals, such as caffeine, increase heart rate. Were you drinking more tea or coffee than usual? Or something else that might have the same effect?

Would you feel similar sensations if you were excited and not anxious? If so, what makes the difference – the feelings or what you make of them?

Easily startled or 'jumpy'

One way that our body prepares us for danger is to make us more sensitive to possible threats around us. So, it is normal for a fearful person to jump at loud noises, but this reaction tends to go when they feel more safe.

Acute sensitivity to sound and vision

Some people are likely to naturally have greater sensitivities to sensations. In addition, being in a state of anxiety can heighten these sensations – it is another way that the body prepares to sense danger.

Tense muscles

Tensing muscles is something that people often do to try to stop feelings of trembling or to try to 'keep in control'. Think, are you tensing your muscles? What would happen if you stopped trying to tense them? See chapter 3.

Aches and pains

Pain is our body's way of telling us that something is wrong. Unfortunately, the pain itself doesn't tell us what the problem is, so it puts us in a state of both pain and uncertainty. It can be tempting to want to be certain about what causes the pain, but this can lead people to fear the worst. What would be more helpful to you – to convince yourself it is something catastrophic just to be certain – or to accept the uncertainty that there might be different explanations, some bad and some harmless? If you *do* know for sure what is causing the pain, and you are taking appropriate treatment, can you accept this and try to focus on other things for a short while? (see also chapter 3 on BMR).

Shortness of breath

Our body prepares for escaping a danger by leading us to breathe faster. It does this by making us feel short of breath, which leads us to compensate by breathing more. Breathing faster and deeper (hyperventilation) can lead a person to feel tingly, light-headed or 'unreal' (see chapter 3).

Tingling sensations

It is a normal response to breathe faster and deeper when anxious – hyperventilation. It is not harmful, but it can lead to unusual feelings. One of these is a tingling sensation, numbness or cramp, often in the arms or legs. It goes after a short while, and this is helped by slowing breathing down.

Lightheadedness, or feeling 'unreal'

This is another effect that can be triggered by hyperventilation that goes with time.

It is also thought that the brain has a way of temporarily blocking out emotional responses if they get too intense. This is called dissociation, and is a temporary phenomenon. It can help to 'ground' yourself on an object, like a squeezable sponge ball, which helps you to focus again on the outside world.

Out-of-body experiences

Out of body experiences are not fully understood. They are often triggered by stressful situations, although not always. They may be a way for our minds to escape feeling extreme emotions, and are another form of dissociation (see above).

Feelings of faintness

Fear usually leads the heart to beat faster, increasing blood pressure, so it is impossible to faint. Sometimes feelings of 'faintness' are actually lightheadedness caused by hyperventilation (see chapter 3). There seems to be only one fear that can lead to fainting – fear of blood or injections. One way to help prevent this happening is to briefly tense your arm muscles when you are about to face the situation, this helps to keep your blood pressure up and so stops fainting.

Feelings of freezing, weakness or trembling

Freezing is another fear reaction. Animals freeze when they think that a predator is near, so the predator cannot detect their movement. Many of us get the same reaction when we are in a situation that we find threatening, even though this reaction isn't that useful for humans. The freezing reaction goes away as the person gets used to the situation.

Blushing

Blushing is a normal reaction that many of us have to feeling at the centre of attention. Have you ever looked at other people to see if they blush? Do people always notice when someone else is blushing?

Pictures or images in your mind

We all experience visual images in our minds, and many people report using them to remember locations and journeys. Some images are memories of things that have happened, whereas others are a result of our imagination.

Distressing images in the mind

Some mental images are more vivid and intense than others, especially if they were experienced at a time of high stress. This is normal – after a trauma it is normal to get intense recurring memories. Mental images are not harmful in any way, but they can often make us feel as though the experiences in our heads are really happening in the outside world.

Crying or being upset

Some people believe that crying is a sign of personal weakness and so they suppress the feelings that might trigger it. Clearly though, when we think about it, this can't be true. We are not usually critical of people who cry after intense trauma, or even after an intense triumph – an athlete winning an Olympic medal. So, it seems as though crying can be a normal part of everyday life. Some people feel that if they start crying they will never stop – could this be true? – have you ever heard of someone who cried endlessly for days and days? Crying is an important sign of being distressed, but is not dangerous in itself.

Getting angry or out of control

People often fear that their feelings of anger are unjustified, should not be expressed, and if they are may get completely out of control. Feeling angry is a normal emotion that everyone experiences occasionally. It is different from being hostile to other people, aggressive or out of control. If this has happened in the past, it does not mean that it will definitely happen again. When people learn to notice and accept their feelings of anger, they tend to get better at responding to it in ways that are more helpful (for example, trying to put yourself in the other person's shoes; or working out a good way of explaining to the person the problems with what they said).

Bizarre thoughts or impulses

Most people report occasionally getting thoughts popping into their head that would be completely out of character for them. These can include the urge to shout out in a quiet place, or to hit someone. It seems that our thoughts do not always make sense.

Thoughts racing

Often, people's thoughts start to feel like they are racing when they have been thinking really hard about things for a long time – it's like you've been pushing a trolley to get it moving and now it's got enough momentum to keep going by itself (but will slow down again after a while). Maybe you could consider how often you need to think things over and over in your head?

Sometimes caffeinated drinks or lack of sleep can lead to thoughts racing, and this is a temporary reaction.

Hearing voices

It is not common to hear voices, but it is not as rare as people think either, and certainly not restricted to people with 'serious mental disorders'. One survey showed that eight in ten people who had recently had a bereavement had heard their loved-one talk to them over the following month. Some people say that their thoughts are often so loud that they seem like voices.

Any change

It is possible for people to get into states of mind in which any-thing they notice seems to capture and draw their attention and frighten them. This can feel very distressing and make the per-son feel very vulnerable and out of control. This state is another form of dissociation and it is temporary. It can help to 'ground' yourself on an object, like a squeezable sponge ball, which helps you to focus your attention on the outside world again. This is a temporary coping strategy that people tend to drop when things get more manageable again.

Appendix 2

The names of the main 'anxiety disorders' and their symptoms

Remember that it is normal to fit more than one of these categories: they overlap somewhat – plus doing things like worrying can keep all kinds of fears going. Your own personal fears may or may not fit exactly into one of these categories. For every one of these categories, the fear and its effects (such as avoiding situations) needs to have an impact on a person's life, or they need to be very distressed about having the fear, for it to qualify as an anxiety disorder.

Specific phobia

The person is afraid of a particular thing – an object, animal, situation – they are nearly always anxious when they experience it, and go out of their way to try to avoid it. The beliefs that different people with phobias have vary a great deal. For example, in claustrophobia the person fears being trapped with no escape. In vomit phobia, the person may believe that they will vomit endlessly if they have certain foods or drinks. Each person has their own individual beliefs about what terrible events will happen if they confront the source of their fear, and this often depends on their own experiences, what they have witnessed, or have been told.

Panic disorder

The person gets panic attacks that come back regularly, some of which seem to come 'out of the blue'. They worry about having another attack in the future. A panic attack involves a sudden rush of anxiety, physical symptoms such as sweating and nausea, and feelings of impending doom. During a panic attack, people often believe that they will die, go 'mad', or lose control of their behaviour.

Agoraphobia

The person avoids situations in which escape is difficult, such as streets, supermarkets and public transport, because they fear having a panic attack and what this might lead to.

Social phobia

The person is afraid of being scrutinised, embarrassed or humiliated by other people in certain situations. The fear may be focused on certain performance situations such as public speaking or interviews, or can be much broader, such as meeting new people or talking to work colleagues.

Obsessive compulsive disorder (OCD)

The person has distressing thoughts that come into their mind that they try to control with repetitive behaviours. These behaviours may be checking, cleaning, hoarding or counting, and they vary between different people with OCD. People with OCD tend to believe that they are responsible for bad things happening to themselves and other people, and that the thoughts they experience make this more likely to happen.

Post-traumatic stress disorder

The person gets memories, nightmares, or physical feelings from a past trauma (a physical or sexual assault, a death or a natural disaster) in which they had experienced fear, helplessness or horror. They are on the alert to danger, try to avoid reminders of the trauma, and often blame themselves for the trauma or how they have coped with it.

Generalised anxiety disorder

The person worries about a wide range of different things and has physical symptoms of anxiety (for example, tension, agitation) most of the time. They find that their worry is uncontrollable.

Other fears that don't normally fall under the category of anxiety disorders that may be helped by the approach of this book

Eating problems

Fear of gaining weight, or changing body shape, leading the person to drastically restrict their eating. Examples of diagnoses are anorexia nervosa and bulimia nervosa.

Fear of long-term illness

The worry that one has a serious, undiagnosed illness that doctors cannot detect. This is sometimes called 'hypochondriasis' or 'somatisation disorder'.

Mood problems

Fear of sudden changes in one's own energy levels or moods (for example, sadness, anger or excitement) that may lead to extreme attempts to control these moods. Some people with these fears may receive a diagnosis of 'bipolar disorder'.

Sleep problems (such as insomnia)

Fear of the consequences of poor sleep, leading the person to worry about losing sleep and to try to control their sleep, e.g. by taking sleeping tablets.

Unusual fears

Many people have fears that are very special to them and few other people would understand. They may involve ideas about certain people, special forces or powers that seem to be communicating to them or targeting them directly. If these fears are severe and have a big impact on a person's behaviour, the person may receive a diagnosis of 'schizophrenia', 'schizo-affective disorder' or 'delusional disorder'. There are also plenty of people who have similar beliefs but because the beliefs don't have a very negative impact on their behaviour, they would not be diagnosed with a disorder of this kind.

'Addictions'

Often, people who use alcohol, drugs, or are involved in certain interests, and find it difficult to give them up, or get control over them. Trying to give up leads to feelings of discomfort, anxiety and other unpleasant states of mind. Therefore, a person can try to cope with the states that are triggered by trying to give up an addiction in a very similar way to the approach described in this book.

Appendix 3

What is anxiety like? Useful analogies for coping with anxiety

Responsibility for coping in other areas of our lives

It is very likely that some of the causes of anxieties and phobias lie with other people, in what they have done to you, or have failed to do in the past, or right now. So, why should you have to be the one who has to pick up the pieces and learn to cope? This is a very understandable response. An everyday example might provide another way of looking at this issue. Imagine you are driving a car and someone else bumps into you, damaging your car. Who is to blame? Obviously the other person – and their insurance will pay for the damage. But who has to contact the insurance company, drive the car to the garage and check that it has been repaired? You do. In this example, even when another person is completely responsible, we accept that we will have to do something too. Could this apply to coping with anxiety?

Imagine your life as a ball of string

Imagine your life as a ball of string, which is lying in an untidy bundle on the floor. The untidy loops and strands are the problems in your life. How would you go about tidying up the ball of string so that you could actually use it? Would you struggle with the messy loops because you can't tolerate them, yanking the string in different directions? If you were to do this, you would probably make the loops into tight knots that were even more difficult to undo, and you might make the string even messier. Alternatively, you could study the string carefully to see where it was looped round on itself, and then gradually feed it through so that it could be wound up neatly. This would take a lot longer, but the end product would be more useful. This analogy shows that we can make our lives more difficult by struggling too hard. Although it might take longer we would do better to study our experiences, try to understand them, and then use some proven strategies to help us learn to cope better with our problems.

Thoughts as clouds

We can all get drawn into our own thoughts, and this is most clear when we are worrying or 'ruminating'. The problem is that getting too involved in our thoughts can take us away from the real world – from what is really happening out there. One technique to deal with this is to see your thoughts as clouds. So when you find yourself thinking about something, try to put that thought into a cloud in your mind, and then watch that cloud as it goes by. It may drift away by itself without you getting caught up in it or struggling with it a great deal. This idea is quite difficult to put into practice at first, but people tend to get better at it over time.

Facing the feelings of anxiety

One approach for facing anxious feelings is to imagine them as a wave. You can't stop a wave or turn it back – but you can allow it to flow past you, and you will come out at the other end.

Learning to cope is a voyage

The sea is a good metaphor for our feelings, and seems to represent them in our dreams. We cannot control the sea; it is a 'force of nature'. Most of us cannot cross the sea by ourselves but we can cross the sea in a boat. The boat doesn't control the sea though; it guards or 'buffers' against it, and moves forward despite the large waves it confronts. Building a boat requires knowledge and raw materials. Similarly, coping with anxiety is a process of building up your knowledge and resources to move on to where you want to go in life, despite the sea, that can be fierce at times. Just like setting off on a journey, you may avoid travelling if the sea is very rough, but you know that to get to your destination you will eventually need to cross the sea. You can practise on short journeys, or when the sea is calmer. The sea is a fact of life, and you can learn to face it.

Appendix 4

A few words ...

You may have noticed that I use particular types of words in this book. I think that it is helpful to be aware that some of the words we choose to use can stifle people's attempts to cope, while others can help them. Here are some words to think about.

Table A.4 A few words ...

Words to never use because they cannot apply to a person, only an object!

wreck	worthless	pathetic	mess	useless

Words and phrases to be very careful using – stop and think 'Is this what I really mean?'

should	must	have to	if only ...	what if ...
why me?	(ir)rational	(il)logical	obvious	commonsense
stop	impossible	get rid of	certain	unforgivable
ridiculous	stupid	perfect	never	always
all the time	I can't believe ...	know	nonsense	everything
nothing	I wish ...	definitely	completely	disaster

Words that seem to help when you use them!

try out	notice	cope	goal	challenge
see	kind	care	uncertain	unhelpful
sometimes	often	feeling	thought	think
reflect	consider	step	build	strength
accept	value	happen	learn	develop
interesting	curious	capable	flexible	understand
experience	possible	sense	journey	discover
helpful	plan	hope	resource	recover

Appendix 5

Further reading

Below are some books and articles that you might find helpful. Generally, they are consistent with the approach of this book, and some elaborate on ideas that I have introduced here. Some also include other ideas and opinions that you can evaluate for yourself. Enjoy the read!

Bob Leahy (2006). *The Worry Cure: Stop Worrying and Start Living.* Piatkus Books.

David Burns (2000). *Feeling Good: The New Mood Therapy.* Avon Books.

Melanie Fennell (1999). *Overcoming Low Self Esteem.* Constable & Robinson.

John Kabat-Zinn (2003). *Calming Your Anxious Mind: How Mindfulness and Compassion Can Free You of Anxiety, Fear and Panic.* New Harbinger Publications.

Gillian Butler and Tony Hope (1995). *Manage Your Mind.* Oxford University Press.

Sam Cartwright-Hatton (2006). *Coping with an Anxious or Depressed Child.* Oneworld Publications.

Helen Kennerley (2000). *Overcoming Childhood Trauma.* Constable & Robinson.

Paul Gilbert (2000). *Overcoming Depression.* Constable & Robinson.

Spencer Smith and Steven C. Hayes (2005). *Get Out of Your Mind and into Your Life: The New Acceptance and Commitment Therapy.* New Harbinger Publications.

Claire Weekes (1996). *Hope and Help for Your Nerves: Learn to Relax and Enjoy Life by Overcoming Nervous Tension* (Audiobook). Thorson's Audio.

And for those who want to read a little wider ...

Allison Harvey, Edward Watkins, Warren Mansell & Roz Shafran (2004). *Cognitive Behavioural Processes Across Psychological Disorders: A Transdiagnostic Approach to Research and Treatment.* Oxford University Press.

Adrian Wells (1997). *Cognitive Therapy for Anxiety Disorders: A Practical Guide.* John Wiley & Sons.

Aaron T. Beck (1976/1991). *Cognitive Therapy and the Emotional Disorders.* Penguin.

David Clark (1986). 'The Cognitive Approach to Panic'. *Behaviour Research and Therapy,* 24, 461–470.

Jack Rachman & Padmal de Silva (1978). 'Abnormal and Normal Obsession'. *Behaviour Research and Therapy,* 16, 233–248.

James Bennett-Levy and colleagues (2004). *The Oxford Guide to Behavioural Experiments in Cognitive Therapy.* Oxford University Press.

Paul Salkovskis (1991). 'The importance of behaviour in the maintenance of anxiety and panic: a cognitive account'. *Behavioural Psychotherapy,* 19, 6–19.

Peter R. Breggin and David Cohen (2000). *Your Drug May Be Your Problem: How and Why to Stop Taking Psychiatric Medications.* Da Capo Press. See also www.breggin.com

Karen Horney (1945/1993). *Our Inner Conflicts: A Constructive Theory of Neurosis.* W.W. Norton & Co.

Or wider still ...

Warren Mansell (2006). *The Bluffer's Guide to Psychology.* Oval Books.

Marvin Minsky (1988). *The Society of Mind*. Picador Books.

Timothy A. Carey (2006). *The Method of Levels: How to do Psychotherapy Without Getting in the Way*. Living Control Systems Publishing. www.livingcontrolsystems.com

William T. Powers (1998). *Making Sense of Behavior: The Meaning of Control*. Benchmark Publications Inc.

Appendix 6

Support groups and organisations

UK

Support Groups

No Panic
93 Brands Farm Way
Telford
Shropshire
TF3 2JQ
Email: ceo@nopanic.org.uk
www.nopanic.org.uk
Telephone: 0808 808 0545

National Phobics Society
Zion Community Resource Centre
339 Stretford Road
Hulme
Manchester, M15 4ZY
Email: info@phobics-society.org.uk
www.phobics-society.org.uk
Telephone: 0870 122 2325

Depression Alliance
212 Spitfire Studios
63–71 Collier Street
London N1 9BE
Telephone: 0845 123 2320
Email: information@depressionalliance.org
www.depressionalliance.org

MIND (The National Association for Mental Health)
15–19 Broadway
London E15 4BQ
Telephone: 0208 519 2122
www.mind.org.uk

Citizens Advice Bureau
Myddelton House
115–123 Pentonville Road
London, N1 9LZ
Telephone: 0207 833 2181
www.citizensadvice.org.uk

UK Emergency Helpline

The Samaritans
Chris, PO Box 9090
Stirling, FK8 2SA
Telephone: 08457 90 90 90
Email: Jo@samaritans.org
www.samaritans.org.uk

Organisations

British Association of Behavioural and Cognitive Psychotherapies (BABCP)
The Globe Centre
PO Box 9
Accrington, BB5 OXB

Telephone: 01254 875277
Email: babcp@babcp.com
www.babcp.com

NICE (National Institute for Health and Clinical Excellence)
MidCity Place
71 High Holborn
London WC1V 6NA
Telephone: 0207 067 5800
Email:nice@nice.org.uk
www.nice.org.uk

United States

Organisations

Anxiety Disorders Association of America (ADAA)
Telephone: (240)485 –1001
www.adaa.org

National Institute of Mental Health (NIMH)
Public Information and Communications Branch
6001 Executive Boulevard
Room 8184, MSC 9663
Bethesda, MD 20892–9663
Telephone: 301–443–4513 (local)
toll-free:1–866–615–6464
TTY: 301–443–8431
TTY toll-free:1–866–415–8051
Email: nimhinfo@nih.gov
www.nimh.nih.gov

National Mental Health Association (NMHA)
2000 N. Beauregard Street
6th Floor Alexandria

Virginia 22311
Main Switchboard: (703) 684–7722
toll-free: (800) 969-NMHA (6642)
TTY: (800) 433–5959
www.nmha.org/infoctr/

Association of Behavioural and Cognitive Therapies (ABCT)
305 Seventh Avenue – 16th Floor,
New York, NY 10001–6008
Telephone: 212 647 1890
www.aabt.org

Emergency Helpline

National Suicide Prevention Lifeline
1–800–273-TALK (8255)
www.suicidepreventionlifeline.org

Canada

Anxiety Disorders Association of Canada
Telephone: 1(888)223–2252
Email: contactus@anxietycanada.ca
www.anxietycanada.ca
Online self-help

Online self-help

FearFighter
CCBT Ltd
3 Kingston Row
Birmingham, B1 2NU
Telephone: 0121 233 2873
Email: enquiries@fearfighter.com
www.fearfighter.com

The MoodGYM
The Australia National University
www.moodgym.anu.edu.au

Index

COPING WITH BIPOLAR DISORDER
A guide to living with manic depression

Steven Jones, Peter Hayward and Dominic Lam

978–1–85168–299–7 paperback £10.99

Coping with Bipolar Disorder draws on the combined expertise of three leading specialists to offer a comprehensive and practical guide to living with the symptoms and effects of bipolar disorder.

Designed specifically for sufferers of bipolar disorder (manic depression), their carers, friends, and family, this indispensable handbook combines definitive coverage of the condition and information about treatment with a new approach that encourages patients to manage their own psychological health using cognitive behavioural therapy, as well as the more traditional medication regimes. The result is a straightforward and readable book which will empower sufferers, in addition to giving them necessary advice on such key issues as sleep habits, coping with stress and anger, and relating to family and friends.

With real-life case studies, helpful chapter summaries, and a full list of support organizations and web groups, this guide will both inform and empower all those who live with the bewildering turbulence of bipolar disorder.

Steven Jones is Reader in Clinical Psychology at the University of Manchester, Academic Division of Clinical Psychology, Wythenshawe Hospital, Manchester, UK, and Honorary Consultant Clinical Psychologist at the Pennine Care Trust, UK.

Peter Hayward is a Consultant Clinical Psychologist at the South London and Maudsley NHS Trust in London, and an Honorary Senior Lecturer at the Institute of Psychiatry, London, UK.

Dominic Lam is Professor of Clinical Psychology at the University of Hull, UK.

'If ever a book lived up to its title, this is it. The clear strategies, tools and techniques presented here with such understanding should make all the difference to those living with Bipolar Disorder – highly recommended.'

STEPHEN FRY

'This is an excellent book ... well-written, comprehensive, practical, wise and empowering.'

DR PETER KINDERMAN, Professor of Clinical Psychology,
University of Liverpool

'This book is practical, realistic, and well focused, emphasizing the individual, family and social resources that can and should be used to deal with a condition as complex as bipolar disorder. Patients and families will undoubtedly benefit from reading this volume.'

Quarterly Journal of Mental Health

COPING WITH SCHIZOPHRENIA
A guide for patients, families and carers

Steven Jones and Peter Hayward

978–1–85168–344–4 paperback £12.99

Specifically designed for people with a diagnosis of schizophrenia, their caregivers, friends, and family, *Coping with Schizophrenia* is an empowering book that sensitively combines factual information and advice with encouragement.

Drawing on the very latest research, as well as their own extensive clinical experience, Doctors Jones and Hayward present the facts of the condition, including definitions and symptoms, the truth (or not) behind common myths, advice on dealing with professionals, medication and its effectiveness, the benefits of cognitive therapy, and much, much more. The result is a uniquely informative and positive book that covers an enormous range of issues and offers those living with schizophrenia the opportunity to play a decisive role in managing and maintaining their own well-being.

Steven Jones is Reader in Clinical Psychology at the University of Manchester, Academic Division of Clinical Psychology, Wythenshawe Hospital, Manchester, UK, and Honorary Consultant Clinical Psychologist at Pennine Care Trust, UK.

Peter Hayward is a Consultant Clinical Psychologist at the South London and Maudsley NHS Trust in London, and an Honorary Senior Lecturer at the Institute of Psychiatry, London, UK.

> '*Coping With Schizophrenia* is a practical, helpful guide on the path toward recovery. It confronts difficult issues in ways that both empower individuals and provide hope for the journey. It offers tools and shared experiences that can help reduce isolation – reassuring people living with the illness and the people who love them that they are not alone.'
>
> KEN DUCKWORTH, Medical Director, NAMI
> (National Alliance for the Mentally Ill), USA

> 'A sympathetic and sensible book, which not only removes much of the fear, loneliness and stigma that surround schizophrenia, but gives up-to-date information and a fascinating overview. It also gives practical encouragement to those faced with such a diagnosis, and their families will find here new strategies and therapies with which to combat this cruel illness and survive.'
>
> MARJORIE WALLACE, Founder and Chief Executive of SANE, UK

> 'This is an excellent book [and] will make a very significant contribution to helping those with a diagnosis of schizophrenia. The book is extremely well written and achieves the difficult feat of combining optimism with realism.'
>
> DAVID R. HEMSLEY, Professor of Abnormal Psychology, Consultant
> Clinical Psychologist, Institute of Psychiatry, King's College London

COPING WITH AN ANXIOUS OR DEPRESSED CHILD
A guide for parents and carers

Sam Cartwright-Hatton

978–1–85168–482–3 paperback £12.99

Is your child frequently miserable or worried? Do they dislike being the centre of attention, or perhaps find it hard to sleep? Do they have a phobia, or have trouble concentrating? If any of these symptoms seem familiar, then your child might be one of the many millions in the world suffering from anxiety or depression.

Coping with an Anxious or Depressed Child uses the latest clinical research in Cognitive Behaviour Therapy to provide clear, effective methods to tackle anxiety and depression in children. Informed by the author's extensive experience as a clinical psychologist and researcher, this navigational tool covers practical issues such as diet and routine, as well as more specialized medical information – from the professionals you might encounter to the prescriptions offered – this book is an A to Z guide for parents of anxious or depressed children, and will help you maximize your child's likelihood of a happy, confident future.

An invaluable resource for the family or the professional, *Coping with an Anxious or Depressed Child* provides the best tools available to reclaim your child's life from the blight of depression and anxiety.

Sam Cartwright-Hatton is Senior Lecturer and MRC Clinician Scientist Fellow at the University of Manchester.

> 'If you are a parent of an anxious child, or you work with anxious children, then this book will answer all your questions.'
>
> DR CHARLOTTE WILSON, University of East Anglia

> 'At a time when access to child mental health services is difficult, and the pressures on clinicians' time are higher than ever, this book will be greatly appreciated both by parents looking for information and practical advice, as well as by child and adolescent mental health clinicians looking for a useful resource to recommend to families.'
>
> DR JAMES MURRAY, Research Tutor in Psychology,
> University of Surrey

> 'This book provides parents with many practical ideas about how to cope with an anxious or depressed child.'
>
> PAUL STALLARD, Professor of Child and Family Mental Health,
> University of Bath